TILDEN
REGIONAL
PARK

TILDEN REGIONAL PARK

A HISTORY

RICHARD LANGS

THE
History
PRESS

Published by The History Press
Charleston, SC
www.historypress.com

First published 2019

Manufactured in the United States

ISBN 9781467142144

Library of Congress Control Number: 2018963522

Notice: The information in this book is true and complete to the best of our knowledge. It is offered without guarantee on the part of the author or The History Press. The author and The History Press disclaim all liability in connection with the use of this book.

To CeCe, Jodie, Tracy, Emma and Juliette, with love

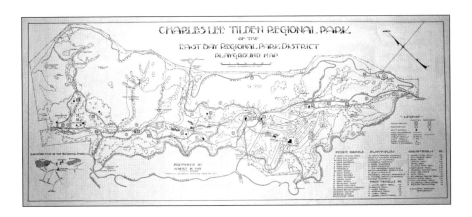

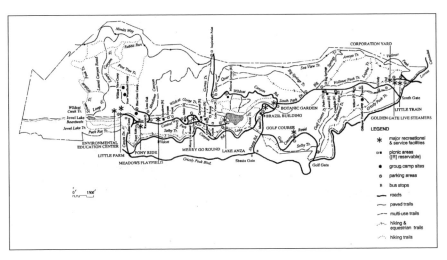

Top: Map of Tilden in 1940 Master Plan. The predominance of horse trails is described in chapter 5, "Along Tilden Trails."

Bottom: Map of Existing Facilities, figure 4 in the EBRPD 1988 Land-Use Development Plan (LUP) and Environmental Impact Report (EIR). Plan's proposals are discussed in chapter 16, "Managing Vegetation and Operating Tilden Park." Note the prevalence of combined use hiking and equestrian trails by 1988. *Both maps courtesy of EBRPD archives.*

CONTENTS

CONTENTS

PREFACE

Tilden Regional Park is familiar to generations of East Bay residents as the crown jewel in a system of seventy-three public parklands that preserves open space, wildlife habitat and historic sites throughout Alameda and Contra Costa Counties.

The park offers a cornucopia of recreational activities: a merry-go-round; a quarter-scale steam train; a botanic garden; swimming, picnicking and camping; and thirty-nine miles of trails for hiking and riding, all easily accessible from nearby towns and cities.

Tilden was one of the first and certainly one of the most elaborate regional parks. But unlike wildflowers after a spring rain, it did not appear overnight. Before Tilden became a park, the area was home to Native Americans, Hispanic ranchos and water company reservoirs for thirsty local residents.

As you enjoy this walk through Tilden Park history, you will discover how public determination, the need for water and the desire for parks converged, resulting in the formation of the first two regional agencies in the country. It's a story about leadership that addressed and resolved seemingly unsolvable problems in order to benefit and serve the public. You will be introduced to many of those leaders.

The city of Berkeley and the University of California were the intellectual centers of the movement to set aside land for public parks. The players were academic and civic leaders who wanted to preserve the area's natural beauty for future generations. Far-sighted though they were, the district's founders would be amazed and delighted at the success of the district today, the largest regional park district in the United States.

After the story of the park's creation, you will learn about the federal government's influence on Tilden Park, first by providing millions of dollars and jobs for thousands of unemployed men and boys in New Deal programs in the midst of the Great Depression. These resources were used to reshape the park's landscape before the public was invited to use its trails. During the war years, the federal government's influence took a new form. With the blessing of the East Bay Regional Park District Board, portions of the park were leased to the military for training and installation of radar stations, antiaircraft emplacements and other defensive facilities that were kept secret and closed to the public.

In the postwar years, general manager Richard Walpole developed new recreational attractions that succeeded in drawing millions of visitors to Tilden each year. Through the 1950s, Tilden was still the flagship park, as the system grew to six parks and six thousand acres by 1954. At this point, the district board and staff were just beginning to learn how to develop and operate an expanding park system. In the 1960s, a new generation of management led by William Penn Mott reorganized the district's structure so it could support an expanding park system, well ahead of the population explosion of the subsequent decades. While the system was absorbing this expansion, Tilden Park, after three decades of over-utilization, underwent a renovation to prepare it for the future.

Each of the district's seventy-three parks, which would total 121,000 acres by 2018, would be uniquely created to protect its natural resources and at the same time provide the recreational opportunities required for the nearly three million district residents. And it all started with Tilden!

ACKNOWLEDGEMENTS

I first met Jerry Kent in 2004 at the first tee of the Tilden Golf Course. Since that time, he has been my mentor in this historical exploration. Brenda Montano of the Public Affairs Department of the East Bay Regional Park District has encouraged my journey for the past fifteen years. Thank you to Robert Doyle, general manager; Beverly Lane, board member; Carol Johnson, assistant general manager of Public Affairs; and Beverly Ortiz, District Cultural Services coordinator.

   East Bay Municipal Utility District: Andrea Pook, thank you for access to EBMUD's archives.

Present and past employees and concession operators of the East Bay Regional Park District:
Botanic Garden: Steve Edwards and Bart O'Brien
Native Here Nursery: Charli Danielson
Nature Area: Alan Kaplan, Dave Zuckermann, Ron Russo, Steve Abbors, Margaret Kelley, Tim Gordon and Sara Fetterly
Lake Anza: Pete DeQuincy
Golf Course: Tilden Men's, Senior Men's and Women's Clubs, American Golf Corporation, AGC Retirees, David Pillsbury, Steve Harker, Trisha Hinze, Ron McQueen, Kevin Shipley and Cal Williams
Merry-go-round: Terri Oyarzun, the Kwasnicki family

ACKNOWLEDGEMENTS

Steam Trains: Ellen Thomsen, Stan James
Federal Public Works Agencies: Alan Kaplan, Gray Brechin (Living New
    Deal)
Tilden Trails: Amelia Marshall, Ned MacKay

To Richard Walpole's daughters, Mel Peters and Mary Granen

To my growing number of colleagues at the East Bay Regional Park archives,
who share my love of park history.

INTRODUCTION

Before embarking on the history of Tilden Regional Park from 1850 through the present day, the focus of this book, I will briefly describe the cultures that preceded the admission of California into the United States. For thousands of years, the first inhabitants of the entire Bay Area, now known collectively as the Ohlone, lived in small villages. Their population consisted of fifty-eight tribes, known by each of the unique dialects they spoke. The small group of people occupying the East Bay coastline up to the hills where Tilden Park now stands was known as the Huchiun.

The Huchiun tribe consisted of between three and five villages of two hundred to three hundred people. The eastern slopes were likely located within the homeland of the Saclan, one of six Bay Miwok tribes. Each tribe's homeland encompassed some eight to twelve square miles of land. The Huchiun and Saclan tribes, like their neighbors, had a deep and abiding relationship with the land that balanced human needs with those of all other species. They managed the land using burning, cultivating and pruning techniques that ensured the health of the plants that provided shelter to a diverse population of animal life.

The Ohlone world was forever changed in March 1772 when the first Europeans visited a Huchiun village located in Strawberry Canyon. Pedro Fages led Father Juan Crespí and five Catalonian soldiers up through the Santa Clara Valley into the East Bay. With characteristic hospitality toward visitors, the Huchiun gave the explorers food and waterfowl decoys and received glass beads in return. In April 1776, another Spanish expedition, this one headed by Juan Bautista de Anza, camped near the headwaters of Wildcat Creek, and the inhabitants of the nearby Huchiun-Aguasto village provided the expedition members with firewood and strings of roasted/dried bulbs.

Unbeknownst to the Huchiun and Saclan tribes, the Anza expedition had arrived to initiate the establishment of a mission, presidio (fort) and pueblo in what is now San Francisco. Between 1780 and 1810, 384 Huchiun and 168 Saclan were incorporated into the mission system, although not without a period of unrest from 1795 to 1797. Ultimately, the introduction of Spanish diseases, to which they had little resistance, and environmental changes wrought by the introduction of cattle, left the Huchiun and Saclan with little choice but to join the mission system.[1]

By the time Mexico won independence from Spain in 1821 and the local governors claimed Alta California as part of Mexican territory, the Huchiun and Saclan ways of life had permanently changed. Although local native people had been promised the eventual return of their land if they adopted Spanish customs, the Mexican government instead carved the East Bay into huge cattle ranches (ranchos) owned by non-Indians. In 1841, Victor and Juan Jose Castro applied for and received land grant no. 550 from Governor Alvarado for the 20,565-acre Rancho El Sobrante. As former soldiers, the Castro brothers were due compensation from the Mexican government. Their grant application was the last of the large East Bay land grants (El Sobrante is Spanish for "the remainder"). The 2,079 acres of Upper Wildcat Canyon, now called Tilden Regional Park, are located in what was the southwest portion of Rancho El Sobrante.

The Spanish-Mexican impact on Wildcat Canyon, then called Arroyo Chico, was the introduction of cattle and sheep onto the rich local grasslands. Even more than for their meat, cattle were valued for their hides and for their fat, used to make tallow for soap and candles. The Castros and the other landowners expanded their trade to the international market, especially the eastern United States, and became cattle barons into the nineteenth century. This was made possible in large part by the unpaid, serf-like labor of local tribal peoples.[2]

In 1846, the U.S. government went to war with Mexico. With the signing of the Treaty of Guadalupe Hidalgo in 1848, the United States assumed military control of California, marking a transition from Mexican to American governance and law.[3] One noteworthy stipulation of the treaty was that all Mexican land grants would be honored. A provisional state government was formed in 1849, and California was formally admitted into the United States in 1850.[4]

BREAKUP OF THE RANCHOS

The transition from Mexican to American law created great confusion. Factors such as legal costs, the land tax burden and the massive influx of new pioneer settlers "squatting" on undeveloped land all contributed to the original rancho owners losing nearly all of their lands.[5]

Rancho El Sobrante was particularly vulnerable, as the original grant contained ambiguous language and loosely defined boundaries. This set the stage for one of the largest land cases in California history. In 1883, after forty-two years of legal wrangling, President Chester Arthur signed the petition defining legal ownership. Lawsuits were filed until 1909, when the final boundaries of Rancho El Sobrante were set and the lands apportioned to various litigants.[6] In what was to eventually become Tilden Park, the court recognized six major holdings.[7] Tenant ranch operations became the dominant use of the land into the twentieth century until private water companies took an interest in upper Wildcat Canyon.

California's first governor, Peter Burnett, declared a war of extermination against native people. In 1850, the California state legislature codified the marginalization of Huchiun, Saclan and other California Indians through a series of laws that allowed Indian children to be kidnapped from their families and bound over as laborers to non-Indian ranch owners.[8] California Indians would not be granted U.S. citizenship until 1924—four years after non-Indian women received the vote.

CALIFORNIA GOLD RUSH AND OTHER EVENTS LEADING TO THE GROWTH OF OAKLAND

Several major successive events caused the town of Oakland to eventually grow into the city of Oakland, which would germinate the growth of all the surrounding communities. The Town of Oakland was incorporated on May 4, 1852. Its growth was related to the establishment of its port as the route to gold country and as a source of lumber for the homes being built in San Francisco across the bay. Oakland's population was still only 1,543 in 1869, when the largest event to impact the region's development occurred: the first transcontinental railroad was completed and Oakland became its terminus. By 1870, greater Oakland had grown to about 12,000 out of a county of 25,000.

Over the next three decades, the town's growth was influenced by the establishment of industrial plants and mills that ran the gamut from breweries to lumberyards and cotton mills, attracting more and more people looking for jobs. The growth of the city was also influenced by the aftermath of the 1906 earthquake in San Francisco when Oakland became a refuge for those fleeing fire and property damage, taking ferries to camp out in whatever open space they could find.

The completion of the Panama Canal in 1914 brought more waterfront development as West Coast shipping blossomed. The United States' entry into World War I in 1917 resulted in increased shipbuilding, heavy industry and shipping of supplies. Several automobile plants were also opened in Oakland in 1917. From these early factories, Oakland became known as the "Detroit of the West." Oakland also earned a reputation as a pioneer in the aviation industry by establishing its municipal airport on Bay Farm Island in 1927, quickly becoming the West Coast terminus for all transcontinental airmail that same year. All these tales of Oakland are described in detail in Beth Bagwell's 1982 book *Oakland: The Story of a City*.

Throughout these years, Huchiun, Saclan and other tribes, although largely invisible to the general population, continued to live, work and maintain ethnic communities. During the civil rights era of the 1960s and 1970s, they began advocating for the protection of ancestral cultural and sacred sites, restoring ancestral cultural traditions and languages and presenting their history and cultures to the public.

The story of the development of Tilden Regional Park, the Queen of the Regional Parks, is a trailhead worth visiting. Read on!

PART I

TWO NEW REGIONAL AGENCIES ARE FORMED

I

HOW WATER SAVED THE HILLS

If not for the need to solve water problems for a growing population, there may never have been an East Bay Regional Parks District or the beautiful gem that became Tilden Park. In the late nineteenth century, the towns of Oakland and Berkeley were growing fast, evolving from farm-based villages with horse-drawn carts into small cities ruled by paved streets, power lines and automobiles. The need for public parks was hardly imagined in this era. Instead, civic leaders desperately turned to entrepreneurs who could divert creeks from nearby hills, build dams and pipelines and bring a fresh and steady water supply to new neighborhoods.

Over seven decades, from 1858 until 1928, private water companies competed to keep up with the expanding population's water needs. As local water supplies neared exhaustion, a public agency was formed to address the East Bay's crisis and to find and develop new sources for water beyond the nearby hills. Just as local reservoirs were drying up, engineers completed a major new water project to bring the precious liquid from the distant Sierra Nevada, providing enough water to support population growth for nine more decades. Ironically, this allowed local and nearby lands that had been acquired and kept free of development by private water companies to be freed up for other uses. Local leaders and average citizens began to imagine a permanent and extensive regional park that could be enjoyed and treasured for generations to come. However, they would first have to get the region's water supply under control.

PRIVATE WATER COMPANIES

In 1858, the California state legislature passed an act stating "any company incorporated for the purpose of supplying a locality with water may purchase or appropriate such lands and waters as might be required."[9] It became possible for individuals to incorporate water companies in order to grab land for real estate promotion and development. A dozen private companies formed to supply water to residents living on the eastern side of San Francisco Bay; they would tap springs, drill wells and dam local canyons.[10] Two of them achieved the most success: the Contra Costa Water Company and the Peoples Water Company.

THE CONTRA COSTA WATER COMPANY AND ANTHONY CHABOT

The Contra Costa Water Company came about through the vision and skill of Anthony Chabot, known as the "Water King." He was a self-taught French Canadian from Saint-Hyacinthe, Québec. Chabot had gained his water credentials in the California gold fields, where he developed hydraulic mining technology; he then used this experience to build San Francisco's first public water supply. While still living in San Francisco, Chabot heard good things about Oakland. It was a small town of 1,500 in 1857; nine years later, it had doubled in population and was soon going to be the terminus of the transcontinental railroad. Seizing an opportunity, Chabot moved to Oakland in 1866 and started the Contra Costa Water Company (CCWC) with the explicit purpose of bringing water to Oakland and surrounding towns in Alameda County. CCWC was granted a nonexclusive franchise by the City of Oakland to lay pipes in the streets; by April 1867, CCWC had laid three thousand feet of water mains. In 1868, CCWC dammed Temescal Creek to form Lake Temescal, located two and a half miles northeast of what was then downtown Oakland. Soon, CCWC was delivering water to local homes and businesses.

Between 1874 and 1875, Chabot built San Leandro Dam in Castro Valley. At the time, it was the highest earthen dam in the world and formed Lake San Leandro (later renamed Lake Chabot). For nearly three decades, Chabot's company dominated Alameda County water production in spite of cutthroat competition from several smaller companies—all of which

CCWC eventually absorbed. But the company was clearly an extension of its founder's inventiveness and business acumen. After Chabot's death in 1888, CCWC lost its dominance to new emerging leaders.

REALTY SYNDICATE, MAHOGANY EUCALYPTUS AND LAND COMPANY AND PEOPLES WATER COMPANY

A second company soon challenged CCWC's hegemony after Chabot's death. In 1895, Frank Havens and Francis Marion "Borax" Smith founded the Realty Syndicate, soon Oakland's leading real estate development firm.[11] One of their concepts was to plant eucalyptus and Monterey pine trees on more than thirteen thousand acres, where they laid out 104 subdivisions, meant to attract families to build homes on the sunny side of the San Francisco Bay.

In 1910, a subsidiary venture, the Mahogany Eucalyptus and Land Company, was formed to grow eucalyptus hardwood on Peoples Company land, including several sites within what is now Tilden Park. When the first trees, planted in 1895, were harvested in 1913, it became clear that the wood

Young eucalyptus plantation on Wildcat Canyon hillside, circa 1911. *Courtesy of EBRPD archives.*

Seedling eucalyptus plants in rows ready for Wildcat Canyon plantation, circa 1911. *Mahogany Eucalyptus and Land Company Prospectus. Courtesy of Marian Koshland Bioscience and Natural Resource Library, University of California, Berkeley, www.lib.berkeley.edu/libraries/bioscience-library.*

warped easily and was impossible to mill for commercial use; the venture was completely abandoned.

Meanwhile, in 1906, the Realty Syndicate purchased the Contra Costa Water Company and reincorporated it as the Peoples Water Company. Whereas CCWC had emphasized developing new water supply sources, the Peoples Water Company's approach was to get demand under control. The company developed the first extensive use of water meters for a major West Coast population when it installed forty-seven thousand water meters. Political forces, however, within the East Bay fought to contain the Peoples Water Company from its inception, aiming to wrest the company's control over the water supply. Politicians and other civic leaders fought all rate increase proposals, especially any attempting to recoup the cost of the meter installation. City councils proposed one buyout proposal after another. All were either rejected at the polls or by Peoples' management, which ruled these proposals as unacceptable to its stockholders. Eventually, these political battles bankrupted the company. Havens was forced to resign in July 1914, and the transfer of the Peoples Water Company to the East Bay Water Company (EBWC) was completed in November 1916.

EAST BAY WATER COMPANY:
TRANSITION TO PUBLIC OWNERSHIP

Water supply continued to be an issue throughout the years of the EBWC's existence. When the United States entered World War I in 1917, additional demands for water were raised to meet the needs of war-related factory operations; the fact that this took place during the drought years of 1917 and 1918 made things worse. The increased demand brought partial water rationing and warnings from state regulators that households must "control use or be cut off summarily." Such treatment was considered harsh by the citizenry and led to a movement toward public ownership of water companies.

Nevertheless, in 1920, Berkeley residents voted down a proposition on the ballot to form a municipal water district with Albany, a bordering city, and other outlying regions in the northern end of Alameda County. The editorial response to this vote was that "such a project should not be imposed piecemeal; all the cities should buy into it."[12] Proponents of the failed ballot measure quickly concluded that passage of any future public-owned water-agency legislation would require a much bigger campaign than that used in 1920.

Edwin O. Edgerton became president of EBWC in 1921. He had previously served as president of the Railroad Commission, the state agency that had been placed in charge of regulating water companies, and was known to favor public ownership of the water supply. Edgerton chose projects that could provide additional water supplies for an interim term, before a larger future supply could be sourced. During his tenure, three new dams were built to create reservoirs in the East Bay: San Pablo Dam, Upper San Leandro and Lafayette.[13] Edgerton also focused on upgrading the distribution system. EBWC would continue to exist while local areas pressed for more control over their water supply and distribution issues.

EAST BAY MUNICIPAL WATER DISTRICT

The state legislature passed a bill in 1921 with a provision to create a special regional district that would include both Alameda and Contra Costa Counties in the development of a reliable water supply to meet growing demand. This would be the first California legislation that ever crossed county lines. First, however, the voters would have to approve it.

Elections were set for 1923. Mayors, commissioners and city attorneys met at Oakland's city hall to enlist support and raise money for a campaign to establish the district and name its initial board. A "Committee of 100" was formed with representatives from business and civic groups appointed to carry on the campaign. On May 8, 1923, after a long and bitter campaign, the proposition passed by a vote of 29,936 to 17,470. Subsequently, the East Bay Municipal Water District (EBMUD) was created and its first five-member board elected.[14] Of the 29,936 *yes* votes, the majority, 21,000, were from citizens of Oakland.

The new EBMUD board quickly assembled an expert team to execute the mission of bringing a new water supply to the district. By August 1923, the board had hired three of America's foremost water engineers to supervise acquisition of this still unknown supply. Arthur P. Davis, George Goethals and William Mulholland were these innovative and well-known engineers.

THE MEN WHO BROUGHT THE WATER

Arthur Powell Davis

Arthur Powell Davis worked for the U.S. Bureau of Reclamation from 1906 to 1914— as chief engineer, then director—until he was hired by EBMUD to serve as general manager and chief engineer. As USBR bureau chief, Davis had been instrumental in outlining the development of the Colorado River Basin before Congress in 1913. He was the first to recommend construction of multipurpose dams whose power plants would amortize the costs of the total project. The dam that EBMUD would construct would be Davis's 100th dam project.

Arthur Powell Davis, EBMUD chief engineer. *Courtesy of EBMUD archives.*

George Washington Goethals

George Washington Goethals was an officer in the United States Army Corps of Engineers in 1907 when Theodore Roosevelt selected him to be the third American chief engineer to attempt the completion of the Panama Canal. Colonel Goethals was tasked with finishing the largest American engineering project ever attempted. He managed the project to completion in 1914, two years ahead of the target date. The project's success was celebrated in 1915 at the San Francisco Panama–Pacific International Exposition. Congress rewarded Goethals with

George W. Goethals, EBMUD engineer. *Courtesy of EBMUD archives.*

a promotion to major general. President Woodrow Wilson then appointed him to serve as the first civil governor of the Panama Canal Zone, a position he held until 1916.

William Mulholland

Perhaps the most notorious of the engineers, William Mulholland was head of the Los Angeles Department of Water and Power in 1902 and was responsible for building the aqueducts and dams that allowed the city to grow into one of the largest in the world. Mulholland obtained the city's water using deception in soliciting land sales and manipulating water rights, along with blunt political force, that led to contentious disputes collectively known as the California water wars. Farmers in the eastern Sierra Nevada's Owens Valley violently resisted having their water siphoned off to Los Angeles. The

William Mulholland, EBMUD engineer. *Courtesy of EBMUD archives.*

223-mile-long Los Angeles Aqueduct, a project that employed over five thousand workers and required the building of 164 tunnels, was completed in November 1913.

George Cooper Pardee

With the three new engineers at work, EBMUD elected George Cooper Pardee as president of its board of directors in November 1924. A native San Franciscan, Pardee was born in 1857, graduated from the University of California in 1879 and achieved his medical degree at the University of Leipzig in Germany. He returned to San Francisco in 1885 to practice medicine and was appointed to the State Board of Health in 1889. After moving to Oakland, Pardee became a dedicated civic leader, first as an elected city councilman and then as Oakland's mayor. In 1899, he became a regent of the University of California and then successfully campaigned for governor in 1903. As governor, he began a program to eradicate San Francisco's outbreak of bubonic plague. Admired by Theodore Roosevelt, he nonetheless turned down an offer to run as Roosevelt's vice presidential candidate in 1904. Following the great 1906 earthquake, Pardee received

George Cooper Pardee, EBMUD president. *Courtesy of EBMUD archives.*

national praise for his ability to muster disaster relief support; he was, in fact, the first governor to request and receive federal aid for a natural disaster. Leaving the governorship in 1907, Pardee served as chairman of both the California Conservation Commission and the State Board of Forestry until he was picked as EBMUD's president in 1924; he served in that capacity until 1941.[15]

BUILDING THE DAM

Between 1923 and 1927, the EBWC was upgrading its water distribution system and constructing additional local reservoirs, while the new publicly owned EBMUD began to focus its attention on long-term supply issues. With its expert engineers and leaders in place, the EBMUD team could begin its mission of bringing a new and more reliable source of water to the East Bay. In September 1924, the Mokelumne River in Calaveras County was selected from among twelve different sources that the new board considered. Next, a funding measure would have to be put to the voters.

On November 4, 1924, East Bay voters overwhelmingly passed a $39 million bond issue that allowed EBMUD to acquire rights and build a dam and aqueduct to bring Sierra mountain water ninety-three miles across the California foothills, the Central Valley, the coastal range and into the East Bay.

In addition to the $39 million bond to build the dam, voters also approved a $26 million bond to support public acquisition through EBMUD of EBWC's assets and distribution system. A seller's market meant a two-year period of negotiations and threats of litigation by both sides. EBMUD finally agreed to acquire EBWC's assets for $35 million on December 8, 1928. The $9 million gap between the money approved by the voters and EBWC's asking price no doubt influenced Pardee's attitude in later negotiations with the park district regarding potential property sales.

While the EBMUD board was in the throes of these intense negotiations, the Mokelumne River project and completion of the Lancha Plana Dam were under extreme pressure due to diminished East Bay water reserves.[16] By June 1929, all the tunnels and aqueducts had been completed and the first waters from the Mokelumne River entered the new Pardee Reservoir, just in time to refill East Bay reservoirs expected to run dry in forty-eight hours.

Ceremony on Pardee Dam celebrating project's completion. *Courtesy of EBMUD archives.*

By 1929, EBMUD had completed the Pardee Dam, one of the largest in the world, as well as the 93-mile pipeline, to solve the East Bay's water supply problems for the foreseeable future. By comparison, the 160-mile Hetch Hetchy project to supply San Francisco with water had begun in 1914, ten years before EBMUD's project, but was not completed until 1934 and cost far more than planned. EBMUD brought Sierra mountain water to Oakland within five years, well within the required timeframe; its total cost, at the time of dedication, was approximately $50 million.[17] Governor Pardee officially turned the project over to the people on October 14, 1929, with his prediction that "the dam will excite the admiration of all future generations."[18]

CONSEQUENCES

One important byproduct of the new water system was that it allowed for modernization of the East Bay's hydroelectric power supply. The Bay Area's energy utility, Pacific Gas and Electric Company, invested $36 million over a seven-year period in the Headwater Power Project, which involved construction of four new power plants along the new Mokelumne River. Completed in 1934, the project did for the electric grid what the EBMUD project did for the water supply.[19]

As a result of the fortunate timing of the arrival of a brand-new water supply in 1929, ten thousand acres of properties would be offered to East Bay cities. It would take numerous individuals, a strong educational and promotional campaign, elections, federal and local funding and a tremendous workforce to create the East Bay Regional Park system at a time when none of these was yet imaginable.

THE CAMPAIGN TO ACQUIRE
A TEN-THOUSAND-ACRE
EAST BAY HILLS PARK

B efore any of the EBMUD lands became available, there were several overlapping and hard-fought efforts to launch a regional park. First, there was the 1930–34 campaign to enact legislation to form an East Bay Regional Park District. Then, in 1936, there was a movement to purchase the first EBMUD properties; among those pieces of land was the long-sought-after Wildcat Canyon parcel that would later be named Tilden Park.

THE PLANNERS

As early as 1866, the hills behind Oakland and Berkeley had captured the imagination of the most renowned landscape architect in American history: Frederick Law Olmsted Sr. Having gained fame as the co-designer of New York's Central Park, Olmsted was brought to California to develop a proposal for the landscaping of the future University of California at Berkeley. Olmsted suggested that parks and "scenic lanes" be developed over the hills adjacent to the new university. He believed that the cost of developing parklands would be offset by increases in surrounding land values and tax revenues. In 1906 and then again in 1915, Oakland city planners advocated using the undeveloped hills as public parks, but no sustained park movement supported these recommendations.[20] One of

Frederick Law Olmsted Sr. *Courtesy of National Park Service, Frederick Law Olmsted National Historic Site.*

the first things that would have to happen was to get the public on board, and groups began to form to enlist popular support, envisioning a perfect park playground for the growing towns east of the San Francisco Bay.

THREE CONSERVATION ORGANIZATIONS

Three organizations formed to ignite a nascent parks movement on a national level and then at state and local levels. Interestingly, all were directly influenced by faculty or graduates of the University of California at Berkeley (UC).

The SIERRA CLUB was the first among these groups, started by professors from UC and Stanford; naturalist, writer and lobbyist John Muir; and others. Muir had gained the support of President Theodore Roosevelt's administration for a National Parks Act, which was ultimately passed in 1916.[21] Stephen Mather, a UC graduate and industrial businessman, was among the leaders of the Sierra Club's campaign to create a federal agency that would devote itself to forming and protecting national parklands.

In 1917, Mather was appointed the first director of a new National Park Service.

The SAVE THE REDWOODS LEAGUE was formed in 1918 by Duncan McDuffie, another UC graduate and Berkeley resident who became chairman of the league's committee on state parks in 1925. McDuffie urged his friend and fellow UC alumnus Governor C.C. Young to expand the California state park system beyond the initial five parks. The movement was rewarded in 1928 by the formation of a state parks commission and voter approval for expansion of the system. Today there are 280 state parks.

The CONTRA COSTA HILLS CLUB was organized in 1920 by UC graduate Harold French as both a conservation club and a hiking club.[22] French understood the need to campaign to preserve the open space in both Alameda and Contra Costa Counties. He described having written "nearly a million words" about hiking, parkland conservation and the necessity to create the East Bay Regional Park District; he was one of its earliest advocates.[23]

THE BERKELEY FIRE

The fire began at noon on September 16, 1923, on the Berkeley side of Wildcat Canyon. A spark from a high-voltage wire that had been toppled by gale-force winds from the north ignited the surrounding dried grasses. Despite the response from the fire departments of all the nearby cities, the blaze could not be contained until forty-five blocks of Berkeley had been incinerated, abated only by the dissipation of the winds that evening. The communities of Berkeley and Oakland were alarmed at how fast the fire had spread, how it had created its own terrifying suction. Most of the damage was said to have been done in just two hours as the fire leapt from grassy areas to wooden residences.[24]

In the days following the conflagration, the fire was described by local newspapers as the forerunner of a war between man and nature. The response of the two main cities affected by the fire, Berkeley and Oakland, was to demand that fire trails and emergency access roads be built. Alameda County's response was to build Grizzly Peak Boulevard from Euclid Avenue to Fish Ranch Road. Construction began in 1926 and was completed in 1932; the road officially opened with two thousand citizens participating in a formal celebration.[25]

GO-AHEAD SIGNAL

On January 8, 1929, Arthur Davis, chief engineer of EBMUD, sent informal letters to the parks departments of several East Bay cities, asking if they would be interested in buying any of the forty-two thousand acres EBMUD had acquired in the purchase of the East Bay Water Company assets. The letters were speculative, as EBMUD had not yet decided to sell these properties.[26]

These letters seemed to be the source of a rift between Davis and Pardee because Davis had apparently not communicated sufficiently with his boss before releasing the offer. This difference of opinion was soon followed by Davis's retirement from EBMUD.[27] Pardee wrote to the cities to state that the final decision, to sell the property to cities for use as parks, had not yet been made. He further stipulated that the land would not be offered to the cities at a discount just because it would be used for parks.[28] Pardee's subsequent correspondence to the cities took an even more assertive tone, warning that a large portion of EBMUD lands might soon be sold to private realtors unless a cooperative agreement with the cities could be reached to purchase the lands for parks.[29]

Davis's offer was a lightning rod for the formation of a series of park associations representing the cities of Alameda and Contra Costa Counties that were ready to participate in the movement to acquire lands from EBMUD and develop a chain of parks in Alameda and Contra Costa Counties. Between 1929 and 1934, five successive committees formed organizations, with different combinations of cities, as support for a regional park concept wavered in the midst of uncertain economic times that deteriorated into the Great Depression.

COMMITTEE NAME	DATE FORMED	PRESIDENT/ CHAIRMAN	NUMBER OF CITIES
Contra Costa Hills Park Association	March 1929	Robert Sibley	Eight
East Bay Metropolitan Park Association	October 1929	Sibley/Roscoe D. Jones	Six
East Bay Regional Park Association	February 1931	Roscoe D. Jones	Nine
Mayor's Regional Park Board	January 1933	Elbert M. Vail	Nine
Citizens Committee of 1000	October 1934	Robert G. Sproul	Seven

ROBERT SIBLEY: CHAIRMAN OF CONTRA COSTA HILLS PARK ASSOCIATION

Robert Sibley, future EBRPD president. *Courtesy of EBRPD archives.*

Already the most prominent leader in the parks movement as a result of having called one of the early public meetings in 1928 to promote a park proposal, Robert Sibley was chosen chairman of the new Contra Costa Hills Park Association in March 1929. He was a graduate of UC and served as professor of mechanical engineering, executive manager of the UC Alumni Association and editor of the *California Monthly* magazine from 1923 to 1949. He later served as a regional park board director from 1948 to 1955. Round Top Regional Park was renamed in Sibley's honor in 1969.

Sibley's initial approach was for the individual cities to pass bond measures to purchase the choicest properties directly from EBMUD. He encouraged the Berkeley City Council to purchase seven hundred acres of Wildcat Canyon and Oakland to purchase Lake Chabot and parts of Redwood Canyon. The Berkeley and Oakland City Councils, in March 1929, placed bond measures on each of their respective ballots to ask voters in May, just two months later, to fund their proposed land purchases.[30] In both cities, the results of the vote on the bond issue were very disappointing. In Berkeley, 55 percent voted *yes*, well below the two-thirds of the votes needed for approval. Low voter turnout was blamed for the defeat.[31] Oakland's bond measure for parklands was more soundly defeated, with only 36 percent of the voters supporting the acquisition. From these initial failures, Sibley and other park advocates were learning what future actions they would have to take to mount successful park campaigns.

ASSEMBLING THE TEAM TO DEVELOP THE OLMSTED-HALL REPORT

Sibley enlisted two members of the association, Berkeley neighbors Professor Samuel May and Duncan McDuffie, to coordinate the survey's completion and ensure it was the definitive document needed as the center point for the regional park movement.

Samuel May

Professor Samuel May received a law degree from Yale in 1913, practiced law for seven years and then received a master's degree in political science in 1920. He came to Berkeley to teach at the University of California in 1921. In 1929, the regents of the university established the UC Bureau of Public Administration as an independent political science research and analysis agency funded by a grant from the Rockefeller Foundation. May was credited with building the finest governmental study agencies in the world in his thirty-four years with the university.[32]

Portrait of Professor Samuel May by Harry Krell, unveiled the night of his retirement. *Courtesy of UC Public Administration Department.*

Duncan McDuffie

McDuffie graduated from UC with a bachelor of science degree in 1899 and later became a well-known residential property developer. His subdivisions, including Claremont Park in Berkeley and St. Francis Woods in San Francisco, were highly regarded for their landscaping. McDuffie employed the Olmsted Brothers firm in planning some of these suburban neighborhoods. He was also known for his civic activism. Cited earlier as an influential member of the Save the Redwoods League, he chaired a committee in 1923 that developed the plan for founding the state parks system. His speech on the subject to governmental and business leaders was praised as "a call to arms." McDuffie

Duncan McDuffie, Sierra Club president. *Courtesy of* Bay Nature *magazine.*

served as chairman of the California State Parks Council from 1925 to 1930. He was president of the Sierra Club from 1928 to 1931 and from 1943 and 1946.

Ansel Hall

Sibley enlisted Ansel Hall, the National Park Service's senior naturalist and chief forester, as a consultant to survey the surplus water district lands to see which properties were suitable for park purposes. After a preliminary reconnaissance, photographing all the EBMUD lands deemed surplus, Hall prepared his initial report, titled "The Survey for the Proposed East Bay Forest Park." He forwarded it to Sibley on May 13, 1930, with a recommendation that further study be undertaken and a budget of $4,100 be provided for its completion.[33]

Ansel Hall, National Park Service senior naturalist. *Courtesy of EBRPD archives.*

George Gibbs and Frederick Law Olmsted Jr.

Sibley, May and McDuffie reviewed Hall's report together and accepted Hall's recommendations for further study. Hall had advised May that he would be unavailable for several months and, since he knew that they were expecting to release the report in the fall, suggested they look elsewhere for an expert. On May 21, Sibley authorized McDuffie to send a telegram to McDuffie's man, Frederick Law Olmsted Jr., the most widely known landscape designer in the country at the time, requesting his bid for completing the park design.

Unfortunately, Olmsted had just finished an exhaustive project with the California State Park Survey.[34] He too was unavailable, as his doctor had instructed him to take two months off in order to restore his health. Olmsted informed McDuffie that George Gibbs Jr., Olmsted's West Coast operations manager, based in Palos Verdes in Southern California, would be available.[35]

Olmsted stated that if Gibbs were hired, he would review and sign off on Gibbs's work. Ansel Hall would also be invited to collaborate in the review of Gibbs's five-month effort, and Hall said he would contribute his

Right: Frederick Law Olmsted Jr., president, FLO Landscaping Company. *Courtesy of National Park Service, Frederick Law Olmsted National Historic Site.*

Below: George Gibbs Jr. (*third from left*) and other members of Palos Verdes office. *Courtesy of National Park Service, Frederick Law Olmsted National Historic Site.*

photographs to the final report. Olmsted's name on the finished document ensured Gibbs was authorized to complete the park design.

By July 29, 1930, the study had begun, even though it was not financed. To that end, Sibley asked Professor May to solicit funding to complete the study. Irving Kahn, president of the Kahn Foundation, donated $5,200 on behalf of his uncle Frederick, owner of Kahn Brothers department store for more than forty-six years. Kahn commented, "My uncle was a great lover of the outdoors; it was one of his greatest pleasures to hike over the Oakland hills and enjoy the inspiring views."[36] Sibley responded to May's fundraising success by asking that he and his Bureau of Public Administration assume responsibility for completing and publishing the final report.

OLMSTED-HALL REPORT COMPLETED

When the forty-two-page report was completed on December 1, 1930, it was titled the "Proposed Park Reservations for East Bay Cities" but unofficially known as the Olmsted-Hall Report. The report concluded that "of the 40,000 acres of surplus watershed lands, ten or eleven thousand acres can be used to create an adequate park nearly 22 miles in length to serve the nine cities of the district." The report noted that East Bay cities had the fewest park holdings when compared to other cities large and small: while the East Bay had less than 1 percent of its area devoted to park usage, other regions devoted 5 or 10 percent of their land to parks. With an ever-growing population of 450,000, the East Bay was undergoing rapid urban development and was ripe for park development.

The report also concluded that the proposed parkway along the ridge adjacent to East Bay cities on both sides of the range would be an important acquisition. It would provide a link in a larger circuit that could ultimately extend around the entire San Francisco Bay, thus envisioning the 337-mile Bay Ridge Trail system that is continuing to be developed today.[37]

EARLY SPONSORS

May enlisted a small group of UC students to solicit prominent citizens to lend their names in favor of the report. Eventually, fifty sponsors were named in the first edition of the report. Dr. Harland Fredericks, who went on to have a career in education as a UC professor and as a political commentator for KYA Radio and KPIX TV, remembered how the group went out to find sponsors:

> We wrote to the president and secretary of every organization in the East Bay cities to enlist their support in getting the public out to vote on the park proposal; most responded offering their help and our sponsor list grew to 1,000.[38]

ROSCOE D. JONES: CHAIRMAN OF THE EAST BAY REGIONAL PARK ASSOCIATION

In 1931, the East Bay Regional Park Association formed a legal team that met with the EBMUD board and urged the district to amend its charter to take on the simultaneous role as both water utility and park board. This team was led by Roscoe Jones, a well-known Oakland attorney with a thirty-year history in public affairs, including organizing the utility district's funding of the Mokelumne project in 1923. EBMUD wanted the parks movement to go through the same legislative and election process the water utility had undertaken. The agency suggested that the park association should create a board that could authorize bond requests in order to purchase and develop parklands. The association refused to give in to the EBMUD position.

ELBERT VAIL: GENERAL CHAIRMAN OF THE MAYOR'S REGIONAL PARK BOARD

Eventually, park advocates changed their position and decided to take Pardee's advice, in essence, to create a separate park district to administer and maintain parklands. A new agency, the Mayor's Regional Park Board, was created in January 1933 with the intention of forming a regional park district. The committee delegates met throughout 1933 to plan how to pass the enabling legislation needed. On August 15, 1933, the board elected Elbert Vail, a delegate representing Oakland, as its general chairman.

CONTRA COSTA COUNTY'S WITHDRAWAL

In June 1934, Richmond citizens started to express concerns about the tax impact of the proposed park district. Both Richmond and Martinez, two working-class cities in western Contra Costa County that had been hard hit by the Depression, rejected the imposition of park taxes and took their views to the Contra Costa County Board of Supervisors in October, just prior to the election. They formally withdrew from the campaign, stating that Alameda County might acquire parklands in Contra Costa County but residents in Contra Costa County must be excluded from park taxes.[39] Alameda County politicians took the position that their five cents per hundred-dollar parcel property tax increase would be offset by a decrease in EBMUD taxes of a similar amount based on assurances by EBMUD, but those assurances were not enough.[40]

DR. ROBERT SPROUL: FORMS CITIZEN'S COMMITTEE OF ONE THOUSAND

Between 1933 and 1934, park promoters formed a citizens committee of one thousand, headed by Dr. Robert Gordon Sproul, to approach every club and public interest group they could find that would support the parks movement, including men's and women's social clubs, the Boy and Girl Scouts, labor unions, the UC Alumni Association and the Sierra Club. They were successful in gathering fourteen thousand signatures endorsing the legislation that authorized the formation of the regional park district.[41]

ROBERT GORDON SPROUL

Robert Gordon Sproul is primarily known for his twenty-eight-year term as the president of the University of California at Berkeley, from 1930 to 1958. His contribution to UC was its

Robert G. Sproul, president of the University of California. *Courtesy of EBRPD archives.*

multiple-campus expansion beyond its much smaller origins.[42] Sproul was an advisory member of the Mayor's Regional Park Association Board. In 1958, he became a member of the East Bay Regional Park District Board and was its president from 1964 until his resignation in 1967. Sproul Plaza on the UC campus bears his name.

THE ROAD TO LEGISLATION

The enabling legislation was submitted to the Alameda County board on August 31, 1934, for certification.[43] State law required a two-step process: the organization would have to receive legislative approval, then public approval. Oakland assemblyman Eugene Roland got the ball rolling by introducing Assembly Bill 1114 in the state assembly. Elbert Vail was chosen to introduce the bill to the legislative body.

The legislation carried an "urgency clause." Supporters had assurances from the federal government that if the bill were signed into law, the green light would be given to fund workers through the Civilian Conservation Corps programs to begin to develop the land. Because the Los Angeles delegation objected to the park district's proposed name, the "Metropolitan Park District," a name the delegation had chosen for its own park system, an amendment was added to change the name to East Bay Regional Park District.

The measure reached the floor of the state assembly and was passed on July 22, 1933. Three days later, the state senate passed it unanimously, and on August 7, Governor James Rolph signed the bill, *the first law in the country authorizing the creation of a park district crossing county lines*.[44]

1934 PUBLIC VOTE

Elbert Vail's leadership in the campaign for the regional park district's formation proved to be critical to its success. Within one year, Vail was able to get legislation drafted, passed by the state legislature and signed by the governor. He then managed the campaign for the public vote.

Park advocates had to get the measure on the ballot of the general election set for November 6. There were twenty-four other ballot measures before the voters that year. Vail and other spokesmen for the regional park district reminded the public that federal and state funds were available to build trails and firebreaks, campsites and roads. The park development would even put thousands of people to work.

Robert Sibley continued to exert his influence in the park movement by authoring a five-page October 1934 article for the *California Monthly* titled "The Chance to Save Our Hills."

On three Sundays between October 21 and November 4, the gates to Wildcat Canyon were thrown open to the public for hikes and picnics.[45] These events were remarkable because since 1928, when EBMUD gained possession of the land and immediately put up barbed-wire fences with No Trespassing signs, guards had been employed to keep people out. It was extraordinary for the citizenry to suddenly enjoy complete access to the potential parklands.

The most elaborate form of park publicity was saved for Saturday, November 3—three days before the election—when a two-hour-long, thirty-five-mile parade was held with hundreds of Berkeley citizens and children dressed in sports costumes. Twelve floats rolled by depicting various recreational activities such as camping, hiking, nature studies, swimming, horseback riding, boating and fishing. The decorated cars, built by SERA (State Employment Relief Agency) workers, started moving at 9:30 a.m. from Fifty-Ninth Street and Telegraph Avenue and proceeded to downtown Oakland, out East Fourteenth Street to San Leandro and then to High Street in Alameda.[46]

On November 6, Alameda County voters overwhelmingly approved the measure by 71.4 percent, with 93,405 *yes* votes and 37,397 *no* votes.

EAST BAY REGIONAL PARK DISTRICT (EBRPD) FORMED

The same ballot provided for the creation of the East Bay Regional Park District Board consisting of Major Charles Lee Tilden, Dr. Aurelia Reinhardt, Thomas J. Roberts, August Vollmer and Leroy R. Goodrich. On the same day the park measure passed, the nation voted confidence in Franklin Roosevelt's "New Deal" legislation by backing Democrats in congressional and state elections.

At the first meeting, held in the borrowed office of the mayor of Oakland on December 10, 1934, Major Tilden was elected president of the East

Bay Regional Park District Board, Goodrich was selected as secretary and Vail was appointed assistant secretary. The next order of board business was to authorize Major Tilden to sign contracts for CCC projects. Arthur Cobbledick, chief landscape foreman for the three CCC camps then established in the area, appeared before the board with plans for work in the proposed parklands still owned by EBMUD; the board immediately approved his plans.

The most difficult challenge facing the new EBRPD was negotiating the purchase of parklands. The bargaining continued for one and a half years. EBMUD quickly eliminated the proposed financing options and announced that it would make 10,000 acres available for sale to the park district for a total of $3 million, or $300 per acre. Tilden requested that the utility district specify which lands were to be offered and at what price. EBMUD responded by naming six parcels of 6,261 acres at a price per acre of $348.[47]

Five independent appraisals were commissioned by the regional park district board, resulting in an average valuation of $89 per acre.[48] Despite numerous letters back and forth, as well as joint meetings of the two boards, there was a contentious eighteen-month standoff between the two organizations. EBMUD president Pardee was called "Pick-handle Pardee" by park advocates, along with a variety of other colorful names, while EBMUD accused the park district of "dilly-dallying."

In later years, Vail blamed the roadblock on a great rivalry between Tilden and Pardee that he believed dated back to their UC years. According to Vail, Tilden was the head of the university band while Pardee led the glee club. "At the time there were less than a dozen girls at the university so the boys went to Mills College for their dates and dances. Tilden liked to tell about the time he learned that the glee club had been invited to a dance at Mills but the band had not." To remedy the situation, "Tilden went over the hill back of the university into Wildcat Canyon and hired the farmer's hay wagon and horse to take the band to Mills. By the time they arrived, Pardee's glee club was serenading the girls. Cutting loose with their drums and horns, the band drowned out the singers. Pandemonium resulted but peace was finally restored with a compromise; the band played and the boys sang."[49]

Although this is a funny story, it is more likely that the deadlock between the two public agencies was primarily caused by financial issues. When EBMUD acquired the assets of the East Bay Water Company in 1928, it was forced to pay a high rate. There may also have been a hint of pique felt by Pardee when he saw the struggle for money to buy parklands being compared to the urgent struggle to fund a water supply. He felt that the need for parks, playgrounds and swimming pools was being compared to the engineering miracle that had brought Mokelumne River water to the East Bay cities in 1929 within days of all other supplies being tapped out.

Franklin Roosevelt's New Deal most likely broke the deadlock when federal funds, to be combined with local property tax revenue, became available for park projects. Even though the voters in 1934 had approved a property tax of five cents per one hundred dollars of assessed value for acquisition and park operations, the park district board didn't have the ability to obtain funding until Alameda County actually added the new tax to the tax rolls and collected funds required by the new park district. Since the country was mired in the Depression, the County Board of Supervisors did not want to increase taxes and refused to allow a new tax until EBMUD agreed to cut its tax by a similar amount.

The park district board resolved this issue by sending letters on November 15, 1935, to each of the East Bay mayors, asking them to advise the board if a $3 million bond measure for the parks would carry their cities at that time. The mayors' assurance that a bond measure would not pass influenced subsequent negotiations.[50] While not what Pardee had intended, a deal was struck between the two regional agencies and the county that would allow the new $0.05 of $100 of assessed value tax to be offset with a reduction in EBMUD taxes that would provide EBRPD with an annual $195,000.

Finally, on June 5, 1936, Major Tilden and Dr. George Pardee issued a joint statement. EBMUD would sell 2,162 acres to the park district to establish and develop the first three East Bay regional parks: 1,900 acres in upper and central Wildcat Canyon, 44 acres in Temescal Reservoir lands and 227 acres of Roundtop (now Sibley Volcanic Regional Preserve). The purchase price was $656,544, or $303 per acre. A cash down payment of $120,000 would precede annual payments of $125,000, out of the $195,000 budget, until the full purchase price was paid.[51] At the same meeting, the park board agreed to provide $63,428 in local funds to qualify for $1 million in federal funding needed for park development projects.

CELEBRATING THE NEW PARKS

A crowd estimated at 7,000 attended the official opening of the East Bay Regional Parks on Sunday, October 18, 1936, at the Redwood Bowl, now located in Roberts Regional Park.[52] "The 120-piece University of California band and 50-member UC Glee Club opened the program, joined for several numbers by the East Bay High School chorus. That was followed by a parade of girl horseback riders from Mills College, St. Mary's and UC and a drill by the ROTC battalion from Oakland, Alameda and UC."[53] Major Tilden was master of ceremonies and the only orator that day. He spoke for a short three minutes about the healthful advantages to be gained through play in the out-of-doors.[54]

However, an earlier ceremony was especially noteworthy for telling the history of Tilden Park. It took place on July 16, 1936, when Wildcat Canyon was officially dedicated as a regional park and renamed Charles Lee Tilden Regional Park. Prominent citizens, including the mayors of Berkeley, Oakland, and Piedmont, along with Berkeley City Council and Berkeley Chamber of Commerce members, were in attendance, although Major Tilden was not. Tilden was on vacation at Lake Tahoe, enjoying the outdoors and celebrating his seventy-ninth birthday and his grandson's seventh birthday.

In the dedication speech, Berkeley mayor Edward Ament acknowledged August Vollmer for putting forward a resolution to the park board that Wildcat Canyon be renamed after Major Tilden, who "had rendered such splendid service in acquiring this park."[55] The tribute to Tilden included a reading of his accomplishments by chamber of commerce president Hollis Thompson. The man who gave his name to the gem of the East Bay regional parks truly deserved this highest honor.

3

FOUNDING BOARD OF DIRECTORS AND FIRST DISTRICT MANAGER

EBRPD'S FIRST BOARD

The directors were authorized by the state in Assembly Bill 1114, and in turn, they authorized and assigned functions to the district manager. The first six board members occupying five board positions were as follows.

Major Charles Lee Tilden (1857–1950)
Ward 5, resided at 1031 San Antonio Avenue, Alameda

Charles Tilden was born in 1857 in a miner's cabin in Chili Gulch below Mokelumne Hill, in Calaveras County, California. Chili Gulch, adjacent to the Mokelumne River, Jackass Ravine and Old Women's Gulch, was the center of the gold country, with a population of about ten thousand miners at the time. Major Tilden's father, Harmon John Tilden, was an attorney before he arrived in California and was soon appointed to several justice positions before backing Abraham Lincoln's successful campaign for president in 1860. He was subsequently elected judge of Calaveras County. Not immune to gold fever, Harmon and four partners reportedly extracted $250,000 worth of gold ore from the mines in one winter. In 1866, with their newfound wealth, the family moved to San Francisco. Harmon Tilden became one of San Francisco's most prominent lawyers, and his son

Left: Major Charles Lee Tilden, EBRPD founding president. *Courtesy of EBRPD archives*.

Below: Board of directors, 1934. *Pictured here are, from left to right*: (*standing*) Vollmer, Stone and Goodrich; also Frank Kittridge (NPS director) and Vail (district manager); (*sitting*) Roberts, John McLaren (landscape advisor), Tilden and Reinhardt. *Courtesy of EBRPD archives*.

attended local public schools. The Civil War turned Harmon into an ardent supporter of Lincoln and leader of the Republican Party in the state. This role enabled him to meet President Grant and many other public figures. Later, Charles would hang a portrait of President Grant in his bedroom, a portrait given him on the day his father took him to meet the president at the White House.

Charles enrolled at the University of California at Berkeley at age sixteen. Four years later, he was a member of the graduating class of 1878 with a degree in philosophy. Charles subsequently entered UC Hastings Law in San Francisco, graduated three years later with a law degree and was admitted to the bar in 1881. He joined his father's firm, which became known as Tilden & Tilden, specializing in title law. The firm had many members of San Francisco's Italian American community as clients, and it grew into one of the largest legal firms in San Francisco.

In 1880, Charles joined the National Guard. With his military training in college, he quickly became a regimental captain. In 1892, he married Lily Francis, a young widow and daughter of a famous Russian water engineer, Colonel Alexander Alexis von Schmidt.[56]

By 1894, his marriage and business interests forced him to resign from the Nationals, but his name was put on the "Life Roll." Two years later, he was a financial and legal advisor to the Nationals and symbolically promoted to the rank of major. However, the Spanish-American War broke out the following year. Tilden wrote that in 1898, "I was picked bodily out of my office and thrown into service at the Presidio." With most of the regular troops dispatched to Cuba—and with the absence of the colonel and lieutenant colonel—Tilden was placed in charge of the San Francisco Presidio, a situation he later described as an "incredible dream."

He returned to active duty as senior major in the First California Regiment of the National Guard, the first regiment of volunteers so mustered in the United States. The unit was sent to the Philippines and took part in the Battle of Manila; Tilden led troops over the Bridge of Spain into the capital of the Philippines. Charles was present when the city fell to American troops. During this period, he earned the lifetime sobriquet of "Major" Tilden: "Practically all the men of the regiment were from San Francisco, and they persisted in addressing me by my military title for the rest of my life."

Major Tilden was amazingly successful as an owner, president or board member of twenty different companies, any one of which would have been enough for an ordinary man. He inherited the Overland Freight Transfer Company from his wife Lily's first husband, Harry Mitchell, and turned it into the most successful short distance transportation firm in the West. He had a large interest in a San Francisco firm that built and repaired cable cars. Through his title law practice, Tilden became interested in real estate and became one of the city's biggest real estate developers. At its height, one of his companies, Gibraltar Warehouse, owned one-third of all the warehouses in San Francisco. Tilden was also associated with an ocean shipping line, a lumber mill, a fruit and vegetable canning business, a dairy farm and an oyster company. "At one time his personal holdings made him the largest individual taxpayer in San Francisco."[57]

In spite of his successes and wealth, however, Tilden knew adversity. While traveling by ship to Europe in 1906 with his family, Tilden was handed a telegram from a business associate when his ship docked in Le Havre, France. He read the first news of the San Francisco earthquake to his fellow passengers and, incidentally, of the ruin of his business. He was forty-eight. He looked up from the telegram and said, "Thank God I'm young enough to start over again," to the cheers of those assembled. When Tilden returned to San Francisco and found his magnificent law library completely destroyed, he gave up his law practice and thereafter devoted himself entirely to a variety of commercial businesses.

The Tildens left San Francisco and moved to Alameda, where they lived until Tilden died in 1950. The family residence, located at 1031 San Antonio Avenue, was originally built in 1896. The wooden eight-bedroom, 4,500-square-foot house was styled after an Italian villa. The home stands today and is one of many exquisite old homes on Alameda's "Gold Coast." When the Tilden family lived there, the property contained tennis and croquet courts, stables and a horse paddock, cutting gardens, arbor dahlia beds and a hothouse. In 1956, the lot was subdivided so that four single-family ranch houses could be built on the property.

Tilden and Lily had six children: Charles Lee Tilden Jr.; two daughters from Lily's previous marriage to Gregory Mitchell, Alexine Gregory and Marion Mitchell; and three cousins who had been orphaned after Lily's brother and his wife were killed in an accident. His six children called him "Papa Charlie." Tilden Way, at the southeast end of Alameda, was named for him in 1946.

Major Tilden often lent his prestige and speaking ability to the EBRPD campaigns, and when he was elected president, his advanced age, seventy-eight, did not seem to make any difference. Between 1935 and 1936, Tilden bankrolled the park district's operations and its first land purchase until Alameda County property tax funds became available. "Tilden spent every Saturday checking on the many federal projects under way." Tilden attended nearly every board meeting, and in his final year as president, he hosted the board meetings in his bedroom, even as he received daily blood transfusions. Tilden carried out his duties with a clear mind and continued to work diligently for the board until 1948, when he finally resigned at age ninety-one. During his thirteen years in office, he was known for his attention to detail and his ability to get people to work together.

August Vollmer (1876–1955)
Ward 1, resided at 923 Euclid Avenue, Berkeley

August Vollmer, Berkeley police chief. *Courtesy of EBRPD archives.*

Born in New Orleans in 1876, Vollmer and his family moved to Berkeley in 1890 after his father's death. Vollmer helped organize the North Berkeley Volunteer Fire Department and was awarded the Berkeley fireman's medal before he was twenty. In 1898, he enlisted in the U.S. Marines and fought in twenty-five battles in the Philippines during the Spanish-American War. In 1900, Vollmer returned to Berkeley and worked at the local post office. In 1904, he became a local hero by stopping a runaway freight train on Shattuck Avenue; the next year, he was elected town marshal.

Vollmer's title was officially changed to police chief in 1909 after he was elected president of the California Association of Police Chiefs. During his tenure, he earned a reputation as the "father of modern law enforcement." He became the first police chief to create a motorized force when he placed officers on motorcycles and in cars equipped with radios. He was also the first to use the lie detector, a technology developed at UC for police work. He required that officers earn a college degree and persuaded the University of California to teach criminal justice, a department that he headed in 1916.[58]

In 1921, Vollmer was elected president of the International Association of Police Officers. He held the position of chief of police of Berkeley until he retired in 1932; during the same period, he organized police departments in San Diego, Los Angeles and Honolulu.

He served as a founding director of the park district between 1934 and 1940 and acting district manager in 1942. His successful advocacy with FDR's administration for WPA funding and oversight of the program's execution was *critical* to the early development of Tilden Park. For all his efforts, the board, on March 26, 1938, resolved that the official name of the highest peak (1,905 feet) in the Regional Park District be hereafter known as Vollmer Peak. Eventually, parks or sections of park were named after four of the five founding board members.[59]

Emery E. Stone (1902–1977)
Ward 1, resided at 2522 Ridge Road, Berkeley

A graduate of UC Berkeley in political science, Stone was called "one of the best known old-time auto men" by the time he retired in March 1975. He started in automobile business in 1923, selling Hudsons and Packards in Berkeley, and spent his last twenty years with Don Doten Pontiac. In addition to his automobile business, he was a director of several banking companies based in Berkeley.

Stone was even better known as a great civic leader. He served as president of many community and service organizations, including the Berkeley Junior Chamber of Commerce, Berkeley Exchange Club, Berkeley Service Club Council, Retail Merchants Bureau and the Berkeley Traffic Safety Commission, and for one year, 1936–37, he was general manager of the Berkeley Chamber of Commerce.

Emery Stone, automobile salesman and civic leader. *Courtesy of EBRPD archives.*

Emery served on the EBRPD board between 1940 and 1948; during this time, he also chaired several wartime and postwar fundraising programs and charities. After the war, he was instrumental in working with district manager Richard Walpole to develop Tilden Park's recreational facilities. He and Walpole toured all the recreational concessions in Griffith Park and made recommendations to the board about which might be popular to implement at Tilden. Stone received the 1949 UC Alumni Wheeler Medal for being the city's "most useful citizen."[60] In 1950, he presided over the

East Bay Metropolitan Planning Council, and in 1953, he was appointed moderator of a committee formed to develop a master plan for the Berkeley City Planning Council. After retiring in 1975, he moved to Balboa Island, Newport Beach. His name is an interesting one: "emery stone" is crushed stone dust that with a binder can be molded into grinding stones.

Thomas J. Roberts (1863–1958)
Ward 2, resided at 571 Sixth Street, Oakland

Thomas Roberts, East Bay labor leader. *Courtesy of EBRPD archives.*

Roberts was a widely known and well-respected East Bay labor leader. In the 1890s, he was president of the Oakland chapter of the American Railroad Union, the nation's largest organized union. In 1894, a nationwide railroad strike was called against the Pullman Company; President Cleveland called out federal troops to break the strike, and the union's defeat lead to its ultimate dissolution. At the time, Dr. George Pardee was Oakland's mayor; he had taken a public position against the Southern Pacific. In 1902, while Pardee campaigned for the governorship, Roberts provided a strong public statement in Pardee's defense in spite of Pardee's anti-union position.[61]

Roberts's civic contributions included a stint as a city fireman. He served twenty-four years as a member of the EBRPD board until his death in 1958 at age ninety-five. He served as board secretary throughout his tenure. Roberts Regional Recreational Area was named after him in a ceremony on October 19, 1952.

Leroy R. Goodrich (1887–1963)
Ward 3, resided at 6028 Broadway Terrace, Oakland

Leroy R. Goodrich was educated in Buffalo, New York schools and graduated from Cornell University in 1908. He entered the publishing business and became general sales manager for the Frontier Press Company of Buffalo.

Leroy Goodrich, sales manager, printing company. *Courtesy of EBRPD archives.*

Goodrich came to Oakland in 1911 to establish and manage the company's Pacific coast office.

Goodrich served as the Republican Party chairman in Alameda County for many political campaigns and was also a leader of several nonprofit organizations. In 1923, he chaired an executive committee dedicated to raising $400,000 to endow Mills College and gave a speech lauding the work of its president, Aurelia Reinhardt.[62]

He was elected Oakland commissioner between 1925 and 1937 (Public Works and Port Commissions) and gave the lead speech at the groundbreaking ceremony for the construction of the Bay Bridge. Goodrich was admitted to the California bar in 1933. Goodrich served twenty-seven years on the EBRPD board, the longest term of any founding member. Among his contributions was leading the board's land negotiation with EBMUD and assuming the leadership mantle when President Tilden was incapacitated.

Aurelia Reinhardt (1877–1948)
Ward 4, resided in the President's House, Mills College, Oakland

After Aurelia Henry earned a degree in English literature at UC Berkeley in 1898, she went on to acquire a doctorate at Yale University in 1905. A year later, she married Dr. George Reinhardt. Only six years later, she was the widowed parent of two sons. She returned to UC Berkeley to teach English. In 1916, she was appointed president of a then struggling Mills College in Oakland and led the college successfully. She was the college president for twenty-seven years, retiring in 1943.

In addition to her work as an educator, Reinhardt worked tirelessly for world peace as early as 1919, breaking ranks with her own Republican Party to support President Woodrow Wilson's plan for the League of Nations. She was a member of more than a dozen peace organizations over the next three decades and served as a delegate to the founding meetings of the United Nations in San Francisco in 1945. Reinhardt took a leadership role in many civic groups, including the American Association of University Women, the

Aurelia Reinhardt, president of Mills College. *Courtesy of Special Collections, F.W. Olin, Mills College.*

General Federation of Women's Clubs' and numerous local governmental commissions.[63] She received honorary degrees from six universities. She served on the park board for eleven years, until 1945. After her retirement, a 735-acre grove of redwoods in Redwood Park was named the Reinhardt Redwood Grove.

FIRST DISTRICT MANAGER

Elbert Vail (1887–1962)
District Manager between 1933 and 1942

Elbert Vail played a leading role in the park's formation. In 1933, he was appointed general chairman by the mayors of seven East Bay cities and led a successful educational campaign in support of establishing the regional park. After playing this pivotal role, he became EBRPD's first district manager, a post he held until 1942.

Vail was born in Japan to parents who were teachers; he came to California when he was twelve and eventually graduated from Oakland High School, where he was president of the class of 1908. He went on to UC and graduated in 1912 with a bachelor of arts degree in economics. As a member of the track team, he held the record in pole vaulting because he was the first to use a light, supple bamboo pole instead of the heavier spruce pole then in use.

After graduation, Vail was involved in parks and recreation at various levels in Oakland, Fort Bragg, Alameda and Fresno, California, and in Fort Worth, Texas. In 1913, he was sponsored by the millionaire brewer Adolphus Busch to travel throughout Europe for seven months to view parks and recreation facilities. Upon his return, he noted that the U.S. facilities were superior.

Vail headed the Travelers Aid Society at the Panama-Pacific International Exhibition in San Francisco during 1915, remaining with the organization until the country entered World War I. He joined the army in 1917, achieved the rank of captain and was given the job of organizing the recreation departments of training camps for soldiers around the country. After the war, he managed the California Chemical Company, which manufactured potash magnesium.

Elbert Vail, district manager.
Courtesy of EBRPD archives.

Vail held the district manager post for the EBRPD between 1934 and 1941 and led the group's interaction with federal and state agencies (see chapter 4). Vail was held to a high standard by these agencies

Vail moving into new park office in Brazilian Building, 1941. *Left to right*: Vail, secretary Georgette Morton and director Roberts. *Courtesy of EBMUD archives*.

and the park board with regard to keeping diligent records and procuring authorizations; he was sometimes criticized by his small staff for sticking his nose into everything. After resigning from the park district on January 15, 1942, Vail represented Moore Dry Dock Company of Oakland before numerous federal boards in Washington, D.C., helping the company to receive commissions to build more than one hundred ships during the war years.

PART II

EARLY PARK
DEVELOPMENT

4

FEDERAL GOVERNMENT SUPPORT
OF REGIONAL PARK DISTRICT

This chapter describes the birth of the Civilian Conservation Corps (CCC) program and how Tilden Park specifically was impacted by this program. It also describes two later New Deal federal agencies—the Public Works Administration (PWA) and the Works Progress Administration (WPA)—and how these agencies contributed to the development of Tilden Park.

The CIVILIAN CONSERVATION CORPS was created by the Franklin Delano Roosevelt administration as a government-sponsored relief program to address the hardships of the unemployed during the worst period of the Great Depression. The new legislation creating the CCC was called the Civilian Conservation Reforestation Relief Act, also known as the Emergency Conservation Work (ECW) Act. As governor of New York between 1929 and 1932, Roosevelt had promoted a similar agency.

Less than a month after his election, and only five days before his inauguration, Roosevelt called a meeting of several key men in his cabinet. Those present included the secretaries of war, agriculture and the interior; the budget director, responsible for personnel management; the solicitor of the Department of Interior; and the judge advocate general of the army.[64] These men would draft the legislation to authorize and create the CCC. For two hours, they listened to FDR describe how the forests needed help to survive and how there were many young American men who needed a "break" to survive the tough economic times.

Participation in the CCC was originally limited to men between the ages of eighteen and twenty-five. Men who were from families on "relief" or government assistance could join as young as seventeen and as old as twenty-eight. Each CCC enrollee received $30 per month, equivalent to $1,440 per month today.[65] The worker was allowed to keep $5 but required to send the balance to his family. Within only two months, the administration expanded the age limit to include veterans of World War I, some Spanish-American War veterans in their late fifties and married men.

The CCC was divided into nine geographic regions. Enrollees from one region were frequently transported to forest camps in another. Federal and state park staffs and the U.S. Forest Service managed the identification and assignment of work tasks while the federal budget department funded the program and took charge of recruiting and selecting enrollees. The U.S. Army was given the responsibility of setting up the camps, transporting the young men, feeding and clothing them and attending to their medical needs.

IMPACT OF THE CCC ON THE EAST BAY

The first contingents of CCC recruits in Alameda County were employed on EBMUD properties in the East Bay hills in the winter of 1933 after having spent the summer months in nearby national park forests.

The creation of the CCC led to overwhelming approval of the measure to create the East Bay Regional Park District in November 1934. Citizens were assured that federal funds would immediately become available to develop the parks and provide fire protection to East Bay communities. This promise was realized on December 10, 1934, when the new EBRPD board authorized President Charles Lee Tilden to sign the contract for CCC projects.

Within weeks of Tilden's authorization, a veterans' camp was begun at Lake Chabot in Oakland, identified as State Project Camp SP-5, or Camp Lake Chabot; each new camp was given a sequential number.

By fall, the Ninth Corps Area Headquarters in the San Francisco Presidio announced three additional East Bay CCC camps that would serve as permanent winter camps: San Leandro Lake (SP-6), San Pablo Dam (SP-7) and Strawberry Canyon (SP-10). The CCC workers were charged with building roads, maintaining forests, setting up firebreaks and other precautionary projects and constructing dams. Two hundred recruits enjoyed tent living in these four East Bay camps, but by the end of the winter of 1933, they had built wooden structures at each site.

1934 RELIEF MODELS

Ansel Hall, coauthor of the 1930 landscape plan used for the founding of the regional park district, continued to support the new district from his office at Hilgard Hall on the University of California campus. In 1933, he had been promoted to chief of the Field Division of Education of the National Park Service and had started developing museum exhibits and other materials to assist interpretive programs for the national parks. By February 1934, he had presented eight-by-fourteen-foot relief maps of the proposed regional park system to each of the mayors of the nine East Bay cities that had been campaigning for the formation of the park system. These maps were the work of young CCC recruits whom Hall had brought to his studios in downtown Berkeley.[66] One of these 1934 CCC maps was restored in 2016 and is on display at the Tilden Environmental Education Center.

Ansel Hall with city mayors and Elbert Vail, 1934 Relief Map. *Courtesy of Smithsonian archives, California CCC Collection.*

CCC CAMPS IN TILDEN PARK

The Tilden Park CCC camp site was situated where the Tilden Little Farm is now located in the Nature Area. Between 1934 and 1941, more than 3,500 CCC enrollees from eighteen states passed through Camp Wildcat Canyon while they served their six-month enrollment terms with extension options. The army provided food, medical care, discipline, education and recreation, training and transportation. The camps were first administered by regular army officers, then later by the reserve officer corps. The National Park Service organized the work. CCC units were frequently relocated in the summertime to national park sites.

CCC Camp Wildcat Canyon. *Courtesy of EBRPD archives.*

FALL 1934 THROUGH FALL 1935

Based in Strawberry Canyon, Company 1238 from Fort Slocum, New York, performed the first work in Wildcat Canyon, beginning in October 1934, opening roads and trails, and clearing fire hazards. Before departing in the spring of 1935, one detachment built the seventy-by-twenty-three-foot education building. Company 3358, with men from Pennsylvania, Maryland and Virginia, continued the work that Company 1238 had started and occupied a tent camp in Wildcat Canyon from April into late 1935.

FALL 1935 THROUGH SPRING 1937

Company 590 was the first to occupy newly built facilities at Camp Wildcat Canyon. More than 200 men from Ohio, Indiana, Kentucky and West Virginia shared nearly twenty buildings, including five barracks where men slept, a mess hall for dining, an officer's quarters, latrines and a bathhouse. The camp also had its own infirmary. Under the command of Captain Morris Orr, the company was responsible for fire and erosion prevention, forestry, insect and pest control and geological work. Company 2712, 170 men from Missouri and Minnesota, occupied Camp Wildcat Canyon from October 1936 through May 1937. By this time, Camp Wildcat Canyon had been designated as the central planning headquarters for park activities for all Central and Northern California CCC camps.[67]

FALL 1937 THROUGH SPRING 1939

In October 1937, Company 5446, 130 men from Mississippi, occupied Camp Wildcat Canyon for a year and a half. Their work record was enviable; they completed over twenty-five miles of truck trails and thirty miles of foot and horse trails with many wooden bridges, performed tree and plant disease control on over two thousand acres of parkland, planted eighty-five thousand trees, constructed forty small dams and removed a large amount of poison oak.[68]

Men of Company 5446, Sacramento District Ninth Corps Area, 1938 Annual Yearbook. *Courtesy of EBRPD archives.*

FALL 1939 THROUGH SPRING 1941

From October 1939 until March 1940, Company 4429, 202 men from Florida, Georgia, Louisiana, Mississippi, North and South Carolina, set to work clearing stumps and planting trees. Stonework was completed on which signs were mounted to direct traffic to new recreational facilities.

In April 1940, Company 5498, with 192 men from Louisiana, Tennessee and Alabama, worked in Tilden and Redwood Canyon. With the help of General Manager Vail and Secretary Roberts and authorization from California legislators, the EBRPD was able to retain men through the summer months to complete the half-finished warden's lodge in Redwood Canyon. They also replaced 100,000 eucalyptus trees with redwoods and pines within the regional park. It was noted that there was enough work to occupy these workers for several decades, but alas, this was not to be. The last task of the company, before departing in April 1941 for the Grand Teton National Park in Wyoming, was to prepare the camp for occupancy by 500 men of the U.S. Army scheduled for maneuvers.[69]

LIFE IN CAMP

Captured in Camp Newspapers

Each camp had its own newspaper written and produced by CCC workers and U.S. Army staff.[70] The October 1938 edition of the *Wildcat* from Camp Wildcat Canyon featured a two-page article by Lieutenant James T. Anderson titled "Army Life." It described the training, duties and opportunities for advancement in both domestic and foreign service and addressed how recruits could progress up the line of command and pay scale. The article clearly outlined a subtle aspect of the CCC experience of this camp for the men who had enrolled in the forestry program, in essence, that enrollees received more than army-level discipline and educational opportunities during the years leading up to World War II. While the war was still an unimagined event for most of these men, the CCC contributed to a military readiness when the United States at last entered the war.

Educational Programs

CCC men were encouraged and given wide opportunities to advance their educations and learn trades. Classes ranged from basic education, such as learning to read and write, to more advanced courses such as journalism. Vocational training covered mechanical skills, operating machinery and woodworking. In addition, men could take classes in photography, dancing, arts and crafts or public speaking, and join a glee club. Camp Wildcat Canyon's curriculum had as many as thirty-six classes that were supplemented by Berkeley High School and the University of California correspondence programs. Learning how to choose from among all the options was considered part of the educational process. When their enrollment terms concluded, the men were offered job placement services as they made the transition back to "civilian" life.

Sports Programs

Basketball and volleyball teams were organized for each barracks for competition with other CCC camps and high school teams. Boxing matches and baseball games were also organized, with individuals and teams pitted against their counterparts in other camps. Winning teams and individual boxers met in public inter-camp field days and in competitions for the annual championship of the Sacramento Division of the North Corps.

Entertainment

The camps periodically hosted dances, plays or musical programs, sponsored by the regional park district or local community groups, where the public was invited to visit the camp or a site selected by the CCC staff. The women invited to these events would be carefully chaperoned. The highlight of the local camps' entertainment offerings was likely the men's occasional weekend pass into downtown Oakland.

CCC LANDSCAPE ARCHITECTS

The state parks division of the National Park Service hired landscape architects to develop designs for the park properties even before the establishment of the regional park district.

Arthur Cobbledick was the landscape foreman who had developed the work plan for the CCC in Wildcat Canyon. In January 1935, he coordinated the building of the master plan for the regional parks. The plan emphasized the need to create proper approaches to the park through the building of roads and horseback trails. In addition, the plan laid out picnic areas and recreational facilities. George Gibbs, no longer Olmsted Brothers' West Coast manager, was another noteworthy planner who joined the CCC in 1934; he became a landscape technician in charge of inspecting seven camps in California.[71]

FATE OF CAMP WILDCAT CANYON

Alan Kaplan, longtime Tilden Park naturalist, described the eventual fate of the former CCC camp structures. "Some of these buildings were in use in the Tilden Nature Area until October 1972, when they were intentionally burned down by the EBRPD Fire Department to prepare the site for the construction of the Environmental Education Center (see chapter 12). Remnants of camp foundations can still be found in the Nature Area. CCC-built structures still in use today are the Jewel Lake restroom, the Loop Road, and various rock-works along the fire roads in the Tilden Nature Area and around Tilden Golf Course."[72] The successful CCC program, which put about three million men to work throughout the country, led to the passage of additional relief programs. All would have a significant impact on the development of Tilden Park between 1936 and 1941.

TWO NEW DEAL FEDERAL AGENCIES
DEVELOP PARK

By 1935, several CCC projects were well underway. In order to secure additional resources necessary for park development, President Tilden sent fellow board member August Vollmer, who had national influence, to

Washington, D.C., although the regional park district still had no agreement with EBMUD on the sale of the water agency's properties.[73]

PWA Request

Vollmer made a presentation to Secretary of the Interior Harold Ickes and his staff in April, urgently requesting $5 million for work projects that would put needy citizens to work and "develop publicly owned natural parklands adjacent to the East Bay cities." Because of the upcoming opening of the Golden Gate International Exposition on Treasure Island, Vollmer stressed that there was urgency for creating a fully functioning park in the East Bay. The world's fair would bring national attention to a Bay Area–wide renaissance, resulting, in part, from federal projects. Among the accomplishments to be spotlighted were the two soon-to-be-completed bridges: the San Francisco–Oakland Bay Bridge and the Golden Gate Bridge.[74] Within days of Vollmer's presentation, California congressman John H. Tolan, representing Alameda County, advised the EBRPD board by telegram, "I see no reason why this project should not move forward as a works relief project and clear up our relief condition," but the PWA had put the project on hold, awaiting President Roosevelt's response to the request.[75]

WPA Request

Tolan steered the request to the newly formed WPA agency, and Thomas Roberts, secretary of the EBRPD board, submitted a request to the WPA for $4.8 million in grants. The application detailed fourteen park district projects, including the building of sanitary facilities, a water system, shelter houses and comfort stations, playgrounds, picnic grounds, a golf course, roads and trails, a rifle range, a boat house, an amphitheater, a yacht harbor, a lake and reforestation projects. The WPA's initial response was to request additional documentation.

WPA Grant

The park district filed a new request with the WPA for a $1.5 million grant to fund fifteen park projects and sponsor a planning staff that would "prepare a master plan and provide cost estimates covering the various proposed features that may be included in the park system."[76] This WPA grant was approved on October 26, 1935.[77] In his 1936 reelection campaign, Tolan boasted that "he obtained for Alameda County more federal money for local improvements, in proportion to the number of people on relief, than obtained by any other congressman in the United States."[78]

BUILDING WILDCAT CANYON ROAD

Even though the EBRPD board had not yet negotiated an agreement with EBMUD on the transfer of the first properties, an arrangement was reached that allowed the WPA work to get started. On November 22, 1935, just weeks after receiving its funding greenlight, the first full-scale WPA project was launched. Five hundred men were put to work building Wildcat Canyon Road, planned to be one of the scenic gems of the East Bay. The road extends from Berkeley near the Summit Reservoir through the heavily wooded canyon, along the ridge overlooking Lake San Pablo, to the lower tunnel road by way of Orinda, a distance of seven miles.[79]

By January 1936, the number of men working on the Wildcat Canyon Road project had grown from 500 to 800. Another 400 were set to work on other park projects. Engineers, transit men and surveyors were engaged in laying out miles of additional park roads. By March, these men were joined by 2,100 from the WPA and 400 from the CCC, all assigned to a total of seven projects that were being sponsored by EBMUD.[80]

By the end of May, the master plan had been completed and WPA administrator Walter P. Koetitz announced that fifteen thousand men had been put to work over the previous six months in completion of a network of roads under the sponsorship of the EBRPD. This included the reconstruction of the Berkeley–Orinda road, which ran through the heart of Wildcat Canyon to the area of a proposed golf course, an area that had been in disuse for many years.[81]

In June, the park district was able to complete the purchase of EBMUD lands for the three original parks, including Wildcat Canyon.[82] With land finally secured, many other projects were launched in 1936, including the beginning of the golf course construction and two more major road contracts.

WPA workers working on construction of Wildcat Road. *Courtesy of EBRPD archives.*

REFORESTATION BEGINS

On March 18, 1937, two thousand redwood trees, packed in moss, arrived aboard ships that had sailed south from Fort Bragg along the northern California coast. Grown by the Union Lumber Company, the trees were destined for the new regional park, the first of several shipments to begin reforestation. Both CCC and WPA workers did the planting, under the direction of John McLaren, superintendent of Golden Gate Park in San Francisco, and Howard McMinn, a professor of botany at Mills College. Both men were volunteer consultants for EBRPD. The redwoods replaced the eucalyptus being removed by the WPA.[83] (See chapter 9, "The Regional Park Botanic Garden.")

NEW GRANTS

Additional grants in 1938 brought in funds to continue with the master plan. One grant brought in $1,075,551.[84] Koetitz notified Vail that the WPA would continue to employ at least six hundred workers and could even hire more in the future. The new grant supported the building of infrastructure projects within Tilden and Temescal and funded parking and picnic areas, lawns, tennis courts and other recreational facilities.[85]

An additional PWA grant provided $233,017 toward projects in Tilden and Temescal Parks, including $100,000 dedicated to building Lake Anza, and $50,000 for the Tilden Park administration building.[86]

COMPLETION OF MAJOR PROJECTS

In the spring of 1939, Northern California WPA work rolls were downsized by 12 percent, or 7,500 people. Nils Aanonsen replaced Walter P. Koetitz as WPA District 8 manager. Meanwhile, WPA work continued. In his year-end summary of work accomplishments in 1939, Vail proudly reported to the park district board that twenty-two major projects had been completed.[87] Crowning the list of achievements were Lake Anza and the new park's headquarters at the Brazilian Room.

Vail continued with his report about the nursery, which had housed fifty-eight thousand redwoods, pine trees and shrubs that were planted in Tilden, Temescal and Roundtop. Furthermore, many miles of hiking and horse trails and six major springs had been developed. A field near the CCC Camp Wildcat had been leveled and turfed for the playing of cricket and other sports; there also were new playing fields near Lake Anza and Camp Padre. Workers had installed water and sewer systems and erected a garage and repair shop. Finally, throughout the park, stone monuments had been built to orient visitors and point out places of interest. Several artistic rest lodges, fireplaces, rustic bridges, benches and picnic tables had been built at various locales in the park.

Two major fires had been brought under control by the quick action of park employees and CCC boys who were on immediate fire call. Vail emphasized the foresight and value in developing fire prevention and suppression facilities within the parks: "They have saved this community thousands of dollars." Vail concluded that these improvements were

CCC-built stone pillars used for park signage.
Photo by the author.

outstanding because of the permanency of the construction and acknowledged that none of this work would have been undertaken were it not for the federal grants from the WPA, PWA and the CCC.

FIFTY THOUSAND MORE TREES

The primary project for 1940 was to plant fifty thousand more redwoods and pine trees, many of them started in the park district's own botanic garden nursery. Planting was accomplished with the cooperation of the UC Department of Forestry, the U.S. Forest Service, McMinn and McLaren.[88]

During 1940 and 1941, the WPA agreed to maintain crews in Tilden Park, augmented by additional workers from the CCC. WPA workers were assigned rock work and paving, grading and sloping, reforestation and construction of trails and picnic grounds. On September 5, 1940, the East Bay Regional Park District was awarded $579,359 to fund additional projects in 1941.[89]

WORLD AT WAR, 1942–44

In January 1942, Vail resigned from the park board, explaining that he felt the need to assist the federal government as it joined in the Second World War. "I feel my knowledge of Japan will be of value at this time," he wrote. The resignation was accepted with regret.[90]

The board then turned to Vollmer to serve as acting district manager until the position could be permanently filled. In March 1942, Vollmer stated that "no vast sums of money are needed to improve the natural beauties of the hill areas," and his exhaustive report to the park board members said "the hill areas should be maintained as a wildwood recreational system."[91] At that point, the nature versus recreation debate as to the function of the EBRPD was tipped toward nature. This balance would be reexamined after World War II. By the end of 1942, all work on the park had come to a halt, and by June 30, 1943, the WPA program had been completely liquidated by Congress.

The impressive facilities that have stood and served millions of park visitors were planned, designed and constructed in record time by a workforce otherwise unemployed during the years of the Great Depression. Each of the special features of Tilden Park deserves its own chapter.

ALONG TILDEN TRAILS

T he earliest ranch roads in Tilden Park were wagon trails used to transport cattle, farm products and quarry rock to downtown markets. The Curran farm, the largest of the farm properties in the area, operated until 1915; other ranches operated until the early 1920s.[92] When the great Berkeley fire of 1923 hit the region, it reshaped the Berkeley hills forever. The response of the two main cities affected by the fire, Berkeley and Oakland, was to demand that fire trails and emergency access roads be built.

ROAD AND TRAIL BUILDING (1933–41)

Federal programs provided much of the early development of Tilden Park, including the creation of roads and trails. Starting in 1933, 3,500 CCC enrollees were put to work building firebreak roads and trails after removing tons of brush and poison oak. In 1935. the WPA funded contracts for workers to grade and surface the park's new roadways and trails. The dual mission of the new parks was to provide a border between nature and the nearby urban communities to reduce fire risk and to provide the entree to exploring the natural world so close to their front doors.

POTENTIAL USERS OF TRAILS: VAIL'S 1936 SURVEY

As the first three regional parks were being officially opened in July 1936, Elbert Vail, the first regional district park manager, prepared a marketing study to identify the expected use of the parks by the public. Hikers were the most outspoken, although their numbers were relatively small. Vail overlooked this group's earlier vigorous advocacy for creating the park district. Although there were six hiking clubs in the Bay Area with 3,100 active hikers, Vail focused instead on the fact that the members of these clubs favored a constant change of program. Hiking was mostly popular beyond the boundaries of the park district, and Vail assumed this pattern would continue even after regional park trails became available.

Vail's report focused on the equestrian groups who used the region for leisure riding. Between Berkeley, Albany and El Cerrito there were nine horseback riding academies that offered riding instruction to the public.[93] An estimated 142 horses were being boarded at these stables. No attempt was made to estimate how many additional horses were kept in people's backyards, horses that were often taken for rides in the parks. In contrast to the rough-and-ready western-style riders from local ranches, the academies instructed a more affluent clientele in the refinement of English hunt-seat riding.

1940 MASTER PLAN

In 1939, a plan for the development of roads and trails in Tilden Park was drafted by park staff in collaboration with the National Park Service. The plan emphasized the recreational uses and enjoyment of natural features of the landscape and asserted that the southern end of the park, where the golf course was already in use, should be available for recreational use and the northern end reserved for the enjoyment of its scenery. The plan was completed and accepted by the district park board as a segment of the 1940 regional park master plan.

The predominance of horse trails (4 to 1 ratio) developed under the master plan reflected Vail's prediction of demand by trail users. By 1940, most of the trail work had been completed by the CCC and WPA. The trail map accompanying the plan listed only six walking trails covering 4.42 miles versus fifteen horse trails totaling 16.83 miles.

Right: Hikers on Tilden Trail. *Courtesy of EBRPD archives.*

Below: Arthur Gore, Helen Capriola (owner of the Kensington Riding Academy). *Courtesy of EBRPD archives.*

HORSEMEN'S ASSOCIATIONS

In the late 1930s, Northern California equestrians were already becoming concerned that the pace of real estate development was encroaching on their wide-open spaces. In Oakland, Mills College Riding Academy mistress Cornelia Van Cress and local businessmen from the Aahmes Mounted Patrol in 1938 formed the Metropolitan Horsemen's Association to promote equestrian presence in the East Bay.[94]

The California State Horsemen's Association was formed in October 1941 with the mission of preserving equestrian trails and hiking facilities on public lands. George Cardinet Jr., who lived on a ranch in Concord, was a key member of this club. He was an activist for equestrian and hiking trail systems. Eventually, the club counted twenty thousand members, including Ronald Reagan when he was governor of California.[95] George Cardinet (1919–2007) would later be remembered as the "father of the California and national trail system" interconnecting open space and parklands, often crossing through different jurisdictions.[96]

THE WAR YEARS (1941–45)

During World War II, military camps were located throughout the park, restricting public access to many roads and trails. The southern end of the park was reserved for the Mount Vollmer Artillery Gun Emplacement and Radar Station. In the northern end, a former CCC camp became an army training and prisoner-of-war facility. These were secret operations that forced the closure of access roads.

POSTWAR YEARS (1946–62)

After the war, the East Bay hills became a popular destination for returning veterans. A small horse ranch provided a residence and a means of livelihood for many veterans and their families. Horse ownership increased greatly in the late 1940s. In Oakland, the Metropolitan Horsemen's Association soared to 959 members in the early 1950s.

Between 1952 and 1962, the Cold War's most intense decade, postwar restrictions were resumed. A site at the end of Nimitz Way was sold to the army for use as a Nike Missile Station, and public access was denied within a two-mile perimeter of the facility (see chapter 10).

Prior to the modernization of the highway approaches to what is now called the Caldecott Tunnel, providing easier access to Contra Costa County in the late 1950s, the hills and valleys east of Tilden Park were still mostly open ranch lands. Cattle grazed both on privately owned ranches and through lease arrangements on water company land. Practically every farmer and rancher kept horses. One of the highlights for all park visitors has been its value as a wildlife sanctuary and the likelihood of encountering deer, raccoons, quail and other birds.

EAST BAY TRAILS FORMATION AND PARK EXPANSION (1962–75)

Twenty-first-century advocates for the Bay Area Ridge Trail credit William Penn Mott with proposing the original idea of a network of trails that would eventually encircle San Francisco Bay, passing through many counties and park areas. Hulet Hornbeck, the district's land acquisition manager from 1965 to 1985, is credited with doubling East Bay regional parkland acreage. Hornbeck was an enthusiastic hiker and a national advocate on behalf of trails.

With George Cardinet, Hornbeck campaigned for Contra Costa County voters to annex their open lands to the EBRPD. In June 1964, the vote passed by a wide majority, and by 1967, the land known as Wildcat Canyon at the northern border of Tilden was acquired. Cardinet then worked with Contra Costa County Republican state senator John Nejedly to lobby for the California Riding and Hiking Trail Act. He scaled up his lobbying to secure passage of the National Trails System Act in 1968 and was subsequently invited to the White House to be congratulated by President Lyndon B. Johnson.

NEW HAZARDS, TRAILS USE POLICIES
AND PARTNERSHIPS

Cardinet and Hornbeck were early adopters of the trails council concept, whereby user groups such as hikers, equestrians and mountain bicyclists conferred with agency representatives to establish trail use policy. Both served as presidents of the East Bay trails council early in its history. Cardinet also advocated for park agencies to formalize staff oversight of volunteer efforts and to create voluntary positions for trail safety patrollers and trail maintenance workers. In his oral history, Cardinet noted that "there is a lot of volunteer work done on trail maintenance, some organized and some unorganized." He especially credited the East Bay trails council and other groups who "have been helpful in organizing volunteers. Every district should have a paid employee responsible for recruiting and supervising the volunteers."[97]

By 1972, trail advocates had formed several regional trails councils. These groups work with state and local park agencies. One result of this partnership was the June 20, 1972 adoption of a "Two County Regional Trail Plan" by the EBRPD. Its main thrust was to develop an interconnection of trails between jurisdictions.[98] In 1973, a rationale for multiuse trails was laid out in the district's master plan for that year and listed permissible activities regardless of trail types: bicycling, hiking, horseback riding, motorcycling and driving off-road vehicles.[99]

In the late 1970s, heavy-tire mountain bikes were invented. At Tilden Park and elsewhere, it became a popular pastime to ride over the dirt trails and rough terrain. Gone was the requirement that bicycle trails be paved. Soon, mountain bikes outnumbered horses in many parklands, and conflicts emerged between the different types of trail users.

Hiking with dogs also became increasingly popular, but the greater presence of dogs on trails added new complications to the multiuse philosophy. Some urban dogs had never seen horses and surprised their humans with unpredictable predatory behavior. Horses can be spooked, not only by dogs but also by such modern inventions as the three-wheeled racing baby strollers that some people introduced to their trail hikes.

RIDERS ORGANIZE THE TILDEN-WILDCAT HORSEMEN'S ASSOCIATION

Jane Binder, a longtime Tilden Park horse rider, recalls the day when she became aware of the conflict. "One day in 1974, Lucile Arnon and I were riding along Nimitz Way and turned downhill on the Havey Canyon Trail. My son Devin, who was about six years old, was riding along with us. 'Look, Mom!' little Devin exclaimed. 'There's a sign that says NO HORSES!'"[100] Sure enough, a sign had gone up, without any input from the community, restricting access to one of the most desirable horse trails in Tilden-Wildcat Canyon Park.

As a result of this conflict, the Tilden-Wildcat Horsemen's Association was formed. Among its founders, and the association's historian, was Esperance "Es" Anderson.[101] Es Anderson recalled the resolution: "We organized a campaign of letter writing and got George Cardinet involved. We sat beside one of these ['No Horses'] signs for a weekend. In two days we collected 35 letters and 656 signatures from fellow trail riders and trail users who protested this unwarranted trail closure without any discussion or public hearings with the people involved." The matter was resolved at a meeting attended by several hundred horsemen. The "No Horses" signs were removed, and most of the trails were opened to everyone.

In a district public hearing on July 8, 1975, the horse people's input was put on record. Equestrians wanted a permanent campsite on a major loop trail to accommodate up to one hundred horses and riders. They riders wanted access to all trails in Tilden and Wildcat Canyon parks. They asked that "Horse Crossing" signs be installed at key road crossings. The riders eventually got most of what they had asked for. Access to trails around the Nature Area would be possible using the Loop Road that had once encircled the CCC Camp Wildcat Canyon. On fire roads, trails would be designated multiuse in general; single-track trails would be restricted to hikers and equestrians. "We asked the horse riders if they would please try to not ride on the Nature Area trails, and to pass the word along," supervising naturalist Chris Nelson reported. "[The equestrians] respected that. After these discussions, you rarely saw a horse on the Nature Area trails."

In recognition of Es Anderson's contributions to the Tilden-Wildcat Horsemen's Association and the regional park district, a popular campsite across from the Mineral Springs Picnic Area, used by equestrian groups since 1972, was renamed the Es Anderson Equestrian Camp in 2001. Es passed away in 2000.

COLLABORATION AND OVERSIGHT
(1980 TO TODAY)

With new hazards impacting riders and hikers on the trails, the leaders of the hiking, equestrian, mountain biking and dog-walking communities began to work together in the 1980s throughout the district. Building on concepts devised by Hulet Hornbeck, George Cardinet and others, these users organized the East Bay Area Trails Council (EBATC) to resolve trail use issues. The park advisory committee, appointed by the park board, considered related questions and made recommendations. The EBATC was an early example of the collaborative approach to directing park policy. Es Anderson (representing the TWHA) was a founding member of the council. In her online history of Tilden-Wildcat Horsemen's Association, she said, "I understand from Hulet that this was the first group of its kind in America. The aim was not only to develop new trails but also to work out trail compatibility."

User groups have also been brought together in recent years around cooperative events, such as the "Tri for the Ridge" gatherings in the 1990s. These brought multiuse park trail user groups together to work on trail maintenance as well as enjoy their common interest in the trails. The park district safety department also trained trail safety volunteers, including hikers, bicyclists, equestrians and dog walkers. Though these efforts have not eliminated all conflicts, they have been effective in educating the public about trail safety rules and providing an auxiliary force for the district police.

The equestrians attempted to extend a collaborative spirit toward the mountain bike community, according to Es Anderson. After a chance encounter on the Seaview Trail with bicyclist Mike Kelly in 1987, Anderson invited Kelly to participate in the EBATC. He accepted the invitation and later that year organized the Bicycle Trails Council of the East Bay (BTCEB). Although the subsequent attempted collaboration between the equestrian and bicycle groups into one council was unsuccessful (EBATC was dissolved around 2003), the bicycle council separately worked with the park district to open seven miles of single-track trails for mountain biking.[102]

VOLUNTEER TRAIL SAFETY PATROLS

Park district staff includes rangers, naturalists and police officers who operate and maintain the parks, offer nature education programs and monitor the parks for safety and public enjoyment. These professional staff members are augmented by the volunteer trail safety patrol, private citizens who hike, bicycle or ride horseback in the regional parks in their spare time. As they enjoy their outings, these volunteers have been trained to provide park visitors with information about facilities and programs, advise them of park rules and report any emergencies or other situations requiring police or ranger attention. They carry maps and extra water as well as first-aid supplies with them when they go out on their adventures. Though patrollers are not police officers, nor are they equipped to handle serious incidents, they serve as additional eyes and ears of the police department. Recognizable by their tan uniforms, the volunteers operate under the jurisdiction of the park's police department.

The district's park operations department organized the first volunteer bicycle patrol. Renee Crowley (who at that time was unit manager for the parkland unit that included Tilden, Wildcat Canyon, Redwood Park and Chabot) remembers that the bicycle volunteers probably started patrolling in April or May 1988. "Generally, I think the bicycle patrol is valuable because we can actually talk to bicyclists on the trail," said Carl LaRue, chair of the group for the past five years. There are still problems with some cyclists using narrow-gauge trails that are reserved for hikers and equestrians. "I end up apologizing for those people," LaRue said, "especially to the horseback riders who are sometimes more upset by such encounters than are the hikers."

Volunteer Safety Patrol logo.
Courtesy of EBRPD archives.

The volunteer hiking patrol originated in 1994 partly due to chance encounters between Officer Joe Furtado and several potential hiking patrol members in Anthony Chabot Regional Park. One was Henry Losee, a San Leandro resident who had been hiking in the park as part of a therapy program to recover from a heart attack. Furtado was in the park, watching for bicycle riders on trails that were restricted to hikers and equestrians. While doing this, he spoke to Losee and other trail users about establishing a hiking patrol.

Furtado had previously discussed such a patrol with hiker Phil Olrich and his son, Matt. As a result of these discussions, Furtado set up an organizational meeting in mid-1994, and the volunteer hiking patrol was born.[103]

In the fall of 1998, the public safety department assigned Peter Volin, a longtime park district employee and former park ranger, to oversee all the volunteer safety patrols. This took some administrative burden off the shoulders of the police sergeants who had been doing the job previously.

Retired public safety chief Peter Sarna has estimated that the volunteer trail safety patrol's value is approximately $1 million per year in terms of avoided payroll costs. "I think the volunteer patrols have been wildly successful," Captain Matt Madison, public safety operations, said. "In fact, we may have been on the cutting edge," he added. "People from across the nation were calling to find out how we were doing things. The interesting thing about the volunteers is that they are out there because they want to be out there. Volunteers tend to be much more dedicated individuals." Beverly Lane, longtime member of the park board, noted that "from the beginning, members of the various Trail Safety Patrols have provided a positive, reassuring presence for visitors in our parks."

TILDEN REGION PARK'S CONNECTIONS TO LARGER TRAILS

Over 150 miles of paved trails connect various East Bay regional parks. Two noteworthy ones intersect with Tilden: the Tilden–Redwood segment of the Bay Area Ridge Trail that was created in 1990, and the East Bay Skyline National Trail, a 32.3-mile trail that links Wildcat Canyon, Tilden, Sibley, Redwood Canyon and Anthony Chabot Regional Parks.

BAY AREA RIDGE TRAIL

The Bay Area Ridge Trail Council was formed in 1989 with the vision of creating the Bay Area Ridge Trail, a 550-mile continuous loop that would eventually trace the ridgeline surrounding San Francisco and San Pablo Bays. Initially a subcommittee of the Greenbelt Alliance, the council has engaged other stakeholder groups, including the Sierra Club and the Trust for Public

Land. The council is also supported by the William Penn Mott Jr. Memorial Fund. Ultimately, the participants want to make Mott's vision of the trail a reality.

In 1989, the National Park Service enlisted Brian O'Neil, the first superintendent of the Golden Gate National Recreation Area, to lead a committee to design the Ridge Trail. One of the first acts of the Ridge Trail Council was to incorporate itself as a nonprofit organization. They advocated that park agencies analyze land-acquisition policy in terms of whether new parcels of land would help complete the Ridge Trail. The first one hundred miles of Ridge Trail were quickly linked because much of the trail was continuous and already part of existing parklands.

According to the Bay Area Ridge Trail website (www.ridgetrail.org), 375 of 550 planned miles of trail have been completed. Half of these trail miles are on public land. The goal, considered feasible, is to complete the entire trail around San Francisco Bay by 2035.

EAST BAY HILLS BENEFIT TRAIL RIDE AND HIKE

In support of regional efforts to create and maintain the Bay Area Ridge Trail, the East Bay Hills Benefit Trail Ride and Hike is held over Labor Day weekend each year. Originally an equestrian event launched in 2001, it is co-hosted by the Tilden-Wildcat Horsemen's Association and the Metropolitan Horsemen's Association. Since 2011, the five-day event has been cosponsored by the Volunteers for Outdoor California. Hikers and riders may use different trails during the day while sharing meals, stories and camaraderie and enjoying entertainment each evening.

TRAILS TODAY

The trail system developed by the CCC and WPA between 1933 and 1940 totaled 21.25 miles. Today, there are 39.41 miles of multiuse and single-track trails in Tilden Park, through many kinds of terrain. These pathways provide access to hikers, equestrians and bikers. With this trail system, Lake Anza, the golf course and other concession-operated activities, the recreational mission of the park continues to be achieved, attracting between 700,000 and 850,000 visitors each year.

6

TILDEN GOLF COURSE

THE DREAM

Roy Butler is credited with being the first to contemplate Wildcat Canyon as a site for a world-class golf course. He got the idea in 1910 when he was captain of the first golf team at the University of California.[104] Butler was manager of the Pacific Nash Motor Company, on Broadway in Oakland, and a member of the Oakland Chamber of Commerce. He later became the first president of the newly formed Tilden Park Men's Golf Club.

In the fall of 1935, the long-held dream of a course adjacent to the university was tantalizingly close. Dewey Longworth, Claremont Country Club professional and coach of the university varsity golf team (1935–40), was in Pasadena conferring with William P. "Billy" Bell over details of the proposed golf links in Wildcat Canyon.[105] The WPA had set aside $130,000 for financing the construction of the golf course and $30,000 for the clubhouse. Work would begin as soon as the land was owned by the park district.

Robert Sibley appeared before the park board in January 1936 to urge that the course be built immediately: "The University of California is the only university in the United States that is not equipped with a golf course and the 40,000 alumni and 10,000 students are vitally interested in its construction," he insisted. He pointed out that the great centers of

Left: Roy Butler, president of Tilden Men's Club. *Courtesy of EBRPD archives.*

Right: Dewey Longworth, UC Golf Team coach. *Courtesy of University of California Bancroft Library.*

population in the East Bay—North Oakland, Piedmont, Central Oakland and Berkeley—would all find this proposed course readily accessible.[106] In all of Alameda County, there were only two public courses and three private country clubs in operation in 1936.[107]

DESIGN AND CONSTRUCTION

The park district finally purchased Wildcat Canyon from EBMUD on June 5, 1936. Just a few weeks later, on June 29, the board gave official approval to preliminary construction plans. Design of the course had already been completed. William P. Bell of Pasadena and his son William F. Bell were the most prolific golf course architects on the West Coast; together, they had created more than 140 golf courses. Bell Sr. was a founding member and later president of the American Society of Golf Course Architects.[108] He and his son were already working under a $2,500 contract with the park district.

Left: William P. Bell, Golf Course Designer. *Courtesy of EBRPD archives.*

Right: Richard Walpole, golf course foreman. *Courtesy of Walpole family archives.*

Course construction began in July 1936, financed by a $130,000 grant from the WPA. Over the next sixteen months, WPA crews would complete major landscaping and construction tasks toward bringing the course into shape.[109] The work involved removing more than thirty thousand trees—mainly eucalyptus, laurel and live oak—using tractors and other heavy equipment. They had to remove forty thousand cubic yards of dirt and then haul in more than eight thousand yards of topsoil and thirty tons of fertilizer. To first seed the fairways, ten thousand pounds of bluegrass were planted, along with four thousand pounds of redtop. The greens were planted with six hundred pounds of kikuyu bent seed.

In June 1937, one year into the job, the district hired a twenty-four-year-old foreman named Richard Walpole on Bell's recommendation. Walpole had golf course development experience, having worked with the Los Angeles Recreation and Parks Department. Young as he was, he was given the job of supervising the WPA crews that were completing their work on the course. It was a dawn-to-dusk, six-days-a-week job. Once seeding was complete, the next steps involved the laying of water and drain pipes

Top: Burning eucalyptus branches as part of constructing the thirteenth hole.
Bottom: WPA workers seeding the green and spreading topsoil in the fairways on
the fourteenth hole. *Courtesy of Walpole family archives.*

and placement of sprinklers; cutting out sand traps and spreading topsoil,
fertilizer and herbicides; blasting a rock ledge on the second hole; building
bridges from the CCC timber supply; and, finally, cutting the new grass
and watering it.

As the course neared completion, Walpole was awarded with a permanent
position as golf course manager and supervisor of operations. On March
25, 1938, Walpole's diary noted, "Vail called and said I would be in charge
of everything" at the golf course.[110]

CLUBHOUSE

While the golf course was under construction, work began on the clubhouse. In March 1937, a $13,430 contract was awarded to the W.G. Thornally Construction Company to build the clubhouse, and work started on June 24. The *Oakland Tribune* reported: "The two-wing clubhouse is being built of redwood logs to conform to the natural rustic surroundings. One of the wings will provide a spacious lounge. The lounge has an adjoining kitchen and manager's suite as well as the grill and fountain service. The other wing will house the shop, rest rooms and locker rooms for men and women."

At the November 1937 board meeting, Dick Sherwood was awarded the restaurant concession, to be renewed each year until 1946. Sherwood completed the restaurant with kitchen and dining room equipment supplied by the district. Walpole thought Sherwood was a "swell" guy.

Tilden Regional Park Clubhouse, designed by Earl R. McDonald and built by W.G. Thornally. *Courtesy of EBRPD archives.*

OPENING PREVIEW

On November 7, 1937, the golf course was visited by fifty players who had been invited to preview the new facility. Among them were the San Francisco Bay Area's four top-ranked professional golfers, four leading juniors and four outstanding women golfers. Included among the luminaries were university president Robert Sibley and Roy Butler. Leonard Thrasher, former Hawaiian golf champion and captain of the UC golf team, made the biggest splash of the day, scoring a hole-in-one on the third hole and barely missing a second one on the eleventh. Despite the acclaim of scoring the first ace on the 140-yard hole with an eight iron, Thrasher lost a few bucks to his playing partner by going in and out of the sand traps while taking a nine on the second hole. Don Haslett, a senior at Piedmont High School, was the winner with a 71; he later became a star player with Stanford University's golf team. First among the ladies was Frances Glover with an 82, one under ladies par. After the first round of play, the reviews of the

More than four hundred invited guests were entertained by Major Charles Lee and Lily Tilden at an informal buffet supper in the Tilden Park Clubhouse following a preview of the new golf course. *Courtesy of EBRPD archives.*

new course varied from "quite tough" to "too easy" and finally "too easy and too tough depending on the hole." All of the holes were considered interesting, especially the par threes, with a few tough par fives to boot.[111]

Regional parks director Leroy Goodrich was master of ceremonies for the celebration held later that afternoon. Dr. Herman Swartz, president of Berkeley's Pacific School of Religion and past president of the Rotary Club, gave a speech commending the efforts of Major Tilden: "We are to be congratulated on the leadership that brought the regional park into being." Swartz then named a dozen civic leaders who had played a part.

Director Aurelia Reinhardt spoke next: "Our work has only just started. We have acquired 2,500 acres of 10,000 acres of natural parklands adjoining the East Bay cities." At 4:00 p.m. Mrs. Charles Lee Tilden Jr. (Lily Francis), assisted by young women from the University of California and Mills College, served supper to the invited guests in the new clubhouse.[112]

PUBLIC OPENING DAY AND FIRST TOURNAMENT

The American Legion formally dedicated the new golf course on November 11, 1937, with a tournament of golfers from twenty American Legion posts for the title of "Legion Golf Champion of Alameda County." The course thereafter was open to the general public.[113]

American Legion Tenth District commander John Beale conducted the flag ceremony and presented the American flag to August Vollmer. T.J. Roberts and Elbert Vail are also pictured. *Courtesy of EBRPD archives.*

PREWAR AND WAR YEARS (1938–44)

Walpole was authorized to hire staff to manage the office as he continued the supervision of the WPA men who were still working on the course. The buildup of public play was hampered for several months by rain until April 1938, when there was finally a noticeable increase in the numbers who came to the course to play.

On April 28, 1938, Earl Nagel was hired as golf pro at Tilden Park after thirty seasons performing a similar function at San Francisco's Ingleside Golf Club.[114] Nagel was recognized for being one of the first men in his profession who felt it was his duty to help youngsters learn the game. He continued teaching children in mass classes at Tilden for the next fifteen years. Nagel also operated the pro shop in the clubhouse between 1938 and 1953.

At the end of 1939, Vail reported to the board that fifty-nine thousand golfers had played the course, a 100 percent increase over the previous year, and the course profit amounted to almost $11,000.

Golfers coming off of the eighteenth hole in the late 1930s. *Courtesy of EBRPD archives.*

Hillside view of the golf course in the 1940s. *Courtesy of EBRPD archives.*

POSTWAR YEARS (1945–68)

The Tilden golf course became increasingly popular after World War II. Richard Walpole, after becoming general manager of the park district in 1945, continued to use his position to exert control over those operating the course. Many people hired during directly or indirectly by Walpole during this time went on to have long and productive careers at the course:

JOHN HOUSTON and his brother Albert managed the pro shop in the clubhouse between 1953 and 1963. John Houston was a veteran Berkeley policeman.

BERT JOHNSON was course manager between 1943 and 1961. He was known for "an infectious smile and a genuine love of people that made golf a better game at the hilltop course."[115]

MAURICE CARPENTER, formerly a British policeman with Scotland Yard, was a park district employee who managed starters working from the clubhouse. Carpenter was responsible for greens fees and for the operation of the old driving range. Known by some as "Our dear Maury," he was one of the most popular people at the course.

Bert Johnson, golf course supervisor from 1942 to 1962. *Courtesy of EBRPD archives.*

RAFAEL RAMOS was assistant manager and starter at the course beginning in 1956, after having been transferred from Lake Temescal. From the age of seven, Ramos was a trained concert violinist, the son of the conductor of the Mexico City Symphony Orchestra. He spent fourteen years touring with his large family in Mexico, Cuba, Canada and the United States. When his father died and the family dispersed, Ramos gave up on music as his livelihood, although he continued working in the arts as a ceramicist and won several awards for his craft at the California State Fair.

ERNEST W. HALL was the superintendent of the course from 1952 to 1963. A native of Berkeley, he served in the war with the Thirty-Fourth Combat Engineers in the Pacific. Hall supervised the upkeep of the course.

AUSTIN DUNN was a revered member of the maintenance crew until he died tragically on June 24, 1949, during an incident in which he attempted to save the life of a contractor. Wilbur Hickman was knocked out when his raised dump truck came in contact with high-voltage wires at the construction site of the new driving range. When Dunn saw the sparks flying, he grabbed Hickman to pull him from the truck, but both men were electrocuted. For his final act of heroism, Dunn's name was memorialized with a plaque located along the walk between the clubhouse and the pro shop. A year before he died, Dunn had caused a sensation when he was visited at the course by Joe Louis, the famous world heavyweight boxing champion known as the "Brown Bomber." It turned out that Dunn had once been Louis's sparring partner.

GOLF CLUBS

Tilden Park Men's Club

Even before the golf course was completed, a group of local golfers met at the Claremont Country Club in Oakland on March 3, 1937, to discuss the organization of a men's club at the new course. By December, they had signed up 56 charter members and agreed to hold the club's active membership to 100 (later raised to 275).

The Tilden Park Golf Club is a group of golf enthusiasts who organize tournaments and enjoy playing competitively. The club plays approximately forty times each year, usually on Sundays, and primarily at Tilden Park golf course. The first club tournament was held one year from the first meeting date—on March 27, 1938. On May 6, David Gray, an Oakland fireman, carded an 84, net 70 to be the first to have his name engraved on the perpetual "Vollmer plaque," still competed for every year. Although the men's club tournaments continued to be played during the war years, the course was generally underutilized. According to some club members, that just gave them a better chance to walk off with a trophy.

Tilden Women's Golf Organizations

Mrs. C.L. Warren was elected president at the first meeting of the Tilden Women's Club on May 5, 1938.[116] The membership, limited to sixty, met every Tuesday, "Ladies Day," at the Tilden Park golf course. The organization disbanded during the war years when the members were focused on war relief efforts.

Its successor club was formed in 1946 and is still active today. It joined the Pacific Women's Golf Association and has played in regional PWGA tournaments every year since. The club's membership enjoys socializing as well as playing serious golf. The club's history, posted on its website, at one time read, "It was a dark and stormy night. The punch bowl was full, the course was playing short. It was the best of times."[117]

Women's Club social event. *Courtesy of Tilden Women's Club.*

Left: Cecil Davis, photographer. *Courtesy of Tilden Women's Club.*

Below: Golfer on the eighteenth fairway, 1950s. *Courtesy of Tilden Women's Club.*

There have been many interesting women members in the club. One was Cecil Davis, a successful freelance golf photojournalist whose 1950s photographs captured the beauty of the early years of the course, before fences and cart paths were installed. Davis was a sought-after photojournalist, said to have made a comfortable living comparable to her male colleagues. A famed "Coca-Cola girl," her portrait graced one of the company's iconic trays. Way too fond of cats, she was called to task for feeding the strays on the course.

Tilden Seniors Golf Club

The Tilden Seniors Golf Club is devoted to men and women golfers age fifty-five and above. The club, started in 1966, provides opportunities for golfers to get together for events and friendly competition. The conference room in the clubhouse was named in honor of Harry Johnson, club president from 1973 to 1997. The club had more than 275 members during his tenure.

COURSE IMPROVEMENTS

New Driving Range

With great fanfare, the course opened its new $50,000 driving range in 1949, located across the road from the clubhouse at the Tilden Park's eighteen-hole golf course. The new layout proved an immediate hit with the golfers, who arrived early to be among the first to take their practice swings. The new driving range was in service for the next eighteen years.

By 1962, the Tilden golf course, then twenty-five years old, was deteriorating and no longer competitive. Many new public golf courses were being built in the East Bay to serve a growing population. Even so, the Tilden course was still a favorite with an average of 70,000 rounds played each year, although this number was down from the 100,000 rounds of the 1950s. An average round now took between six and eight hours to play.

The Nine-Hole Course

The idea for this course came from the board's golf course committee, who argued that novice players caused most of the slowdown in play; the board recommended that a nine-hole golf course be constructed adjoining the present course in order to alleviate this problem. Noted golf course architect Robert Graves was hired to create a plan for a site near the course on Wildcat Canyon Road, just above the Mineral Springs campsite. The course was to have short and long tees for each hole and be a par 27, 1,320 yards long on the normal tees and 1,505 yards long and a par 28 on the long tees.[118]

The new course was partially financed by a $0.25 surcharge on each round of golf played at the eighteen-hole course. Over the three years that this fee was imposed (1963 to 1966), it netted nearly $30,000. A total of about $140,000 was spent on design and construction before the project was put on hold in 1967, when the course was 50 percent complete. Upon the recommendation of the committee's golf course consultant, the nine-hole course was abandoned in 1968, and resources were shifted toward making the existing eighteen-hole course more successful. Remnants of the nine-hole course can still be found above the Es Anderson Equestrian Camp site on Wildcat Road.

Pro Shop, Driving Range and First Tee

Other projects undertaken at this time proved more successful. One was the pro shop, constructed at the back of the first tee above and to the right of the area where the new driving range would later be built. To accommodate these changes, the first hole tee area had to be rebuilt, shortening the hole from a par 5, 450 yards, to the par 4, 411-yard hole that exists today.

The new pro shop opened in the spring of 1966, and the new driving range was completed in March 1967.[119] The cost of both projects was $79,000. The new driving range with its three-hundred-yard length was touted by the park district as "the longest and most modern in the Bay Area." After the new driving range was completed, the former range was demolished and the area was eventually leased by the park district to the California Native Plant Society. The first gas-powered golf carts were deployed in 1967, although cart paths had not yet been constructed.

In 1965, with the new pro shop under construction on the first tee, the responsibilities of the pro shop concessionaires were expanded to include collecting greens fees, providing starters and handling golf course reservations. Operation of the new shop was put out to competitive bid, and a series of concessionaires operated it between 1963 and 1971.

Other Changes

While the collection of greens fees had been transferred to concession operators, the task of improving the golf course itself was still the responsibility of the park district's golf course superintendent. Jerry Kent had the job from 1965 to 1967, until Lee Huang took over from 1967 to 1971. One of Kent's first acts was to inform the board that $121,000 was needed over the next five to eight years to repair the drainage and surface of tees and greens in order to improve slow play. One major change was to carve out the upper half of the hillside on the fourth hole (now the third hole), so that the fairway below it was visible. Previously, as many as four groups would congregate there, waiting for the signal from a forecaddie that it was clear to tee off.

CALL FOR A SINGLE CONCESSIONAIRE TO OPERATE THE COURSE

In 1968, golf course consultants William Sherman and Associates were hired by the park board to make recommendations for course improvements.[120] They produced a ninety-two-page report that estimated that the cost of rejuvenating the thirty-one-year-old course would be about $500,000. The board concluded that the district did not have the funds to upgrade the golf course and asked staff to pursue the option of attracting a private golf operator that could take over the operation and rehabilitation of the course. Board member John MacDonald summed the situation up succinctly in 1970, saying, "After 35 years we decided we don't know anything about running a golf course." [121]

DON THE BEACHCOMBER ENTERPRISES

Sandy Burns, AGC vice president and golf division general manager. *Courtesy American Golf Corporation.*

Between June 1970 and February 1971, twenty candidates were vetted, and only one was classified as a qualified bidder. Don the Beachcomber Enterprises operated Polynesian-style restaurants and ran properties for residential use and leisure time activities. Its golf division, created in 1965, operated two Los Angeles courses prior to leasing Tilden Regional Park's golf course. The board voted to award the lease to Don the Beachcomber. After the lease was signed, about thirteen or fourteen park employees were transferred from the golf course to positions in other regional parks.[122]

E.C. "Sandy" Burns was vice president of Don the Beachcomber Enterprises and general manager of the golf division. Burns developed the successful lease proposal and brought in Don Morrison as golf course manager and Richard Bermudez as superintendent.[123] Burns remained active in Tilden Golf Course's redevelopment, overseeing progress as he also continued to acquire other golf courses.

AMERICAN GOLF CORPORATION

As the enterprise expanded its holdings of golf course operations, it changed its name twice, first to California Golf Corporation and then, as it expanded beyond the borders of the state, to the American Golf Corporation (AGC). AGC became the world's largest golf course management company with over three hundred courses and nineteen thousand employees at its peak. After the financial meltdown in 2008, the company's ownership was forced to downsize, and AGC now operates about eighty golf courses and resorts in the United States. The relationship between the regional park and AGC is now in its forty-eighth year.

EARLY COURSE IMPROVEMENTS

Under the terms of the 1971 agreement, $500,000 worth of improvements was required during the first five years of the lease. After these goals were quickly met, the course continued to make improvements. Among them was the installation of golf paths for the entire course. A 1974 report had indicated that many people did not want to walk the full golf course, so Burns generated a project with $50,000 to create paved walkways.

GRADUAL COURSE DETERIORATION AND AN UPSWING

After the improvements made in the 1970s, there were no new major improvement projects for the next three decades. A new lease was signed in 1985 calling for a gradual increase in rates to finance improvements, but whether it was insufficient revenue or the decision of American Golf's leadership, for the next ten years, few improvements were made. Renee Crowley, Tilden Park's unit manager at that time, commented in a 2007 interview: "From 1986 [when I started] to 1995, American Golf wasn't putting any money into Tilden."[124]

HISTORY OF "THE TEAM"

In 1996, when David Pillsbury took over leadership of American Golf's northern region, which included Tilden Park, he recognized how fragile the relationship had become. He started serious discussions with the park district's assistant general manager, Jerry Kent. Pillsbury was excited to make Tilden a flagship golf course in Northern California and wanted to explore the possibilities of showcasing the course. In 1996, Pillsbury brought in Sam Singh as superintendent. Cam Stephens became Tilden's general manager in 1997. The team of David Pillsbury, Cam Stephens and Sam Singh made things happen. Stephens was young, and this was his first assignment. Singh coached him about working with the park district, being patient and giving them the time and attention needed. This team developed amendments to the 1985 lease agreement, which included a rate structure to capture more income to contribute to the cost of improvements that would be jointly financed by the park district and AGC.

In Phase I, $2.5 million was allocated for course and clubhouse improvements. The most significant of these improvements would be the construction of a new triple-tiered driving range and a nine-thousand-square-foot putting green. Other improvements included bridge replacements, concrete cart paths, a resurfaced parking lot and programs for drainage and tree trimming. A grand celebration was held on November 27, 1998,

David Pillsbury, AGC regional manager/president. *Photo by the author.*

to showcase the completion of the new driving range. The Phase II Renovation Program covered the years of 1999 through 2003 and gave its highest priority to creek restoration, irrigation system replacement and drainage upgrades. A $2.4 million investment was planned for these course improvements.

David Pillsbury enjoyed a fourteen-year career with American Golf Corporation and became president in 1997. He played a key role in the $1.1 billion sale of the company in 2003. In 2006, Pillsbury was appointed president of PGA Tour Golf Course Properties and had other executive positions with the company. He left the golf industry in 2015 to be president of Laser Spine Institute, a leader in minimally invasive spine surgery.

GOLF PROFESSIONAL STAFF

Golf Course Managers

Cal Williams, Tilden Regional Park golf course manager. *Photo by the author.*

In the last eighteen years, the course has had six course managers. Marc Souza, John Theilade, Jenny Duce, Shelley Hara and Brian Catalli preceded Cal Williams, who serves both as the current course manager at Tilden Park and as AGC regional manager for Northern California public courses. Cal previously worked at AGC courses in Staten Island and Atlanta.

Trisha Hinze

Trish is Tilden Park golf course's PGA director of instruction and has been part of the Tilden staff since 1985. She started working at Tilden as a student at UC Berkeley and after graduation decided to stay. Trish has made Tilden one of the top ten women-friendly and welcoming courses in the country. She has been ranked among the top women professional golfers

in Northern California. She started playing as an eight-year-old in Waterloo, Iowa. Her older brothers were golf fanatics, happy to teach their little sister how to play. "It was either that or be left behind at home during the summer, and it worked out great because I developed a great relationship with my brothers."[125]

The instruction program run by Trish and her assistant Ron McQueen is part of the Bay Area Learning Centers and caters to adults and juniors. It is especially active in the summer when junior camps fill the course with boys and girls carrying little golf bags and learning the rules of the game and how to hit the ball.

Trish Hinze, Tilden Regional Park director of instruction. *Photo by the author.*

Superintendents

Since 2000, the course has been under the care of four superintendents. Matt Wisely, Rodney Muller and Jay Neunsinger preceded current superintendent Kevin Shipley. Kevin got his start as an assistant superintendent in Bend, Oregon. He had the superintendent position at two Troon golf courses, Maderas Golf Club and Carmel Highlands Golf Resort in San Diego, before coming to Tilden in 2015. Under Kevin's tenure, Tilden golf course has been certified by the Audubon International Cooperative Sanctuary Program as having met all the standards for the protection of both the environment and natural wildlife.

Kevin Shipley, Tilden Regional Park golf course superintendent. *Photo by the author.*

AMBASSADOR PROGRAM AND
AMERICAN GOLF FOUNDATION

The Ambassador Program was formulated in 1985 with the goal of helping golfers to enjoy the golf experience by educating them regarding proper course etiquette, safety and pace of play. Leon Rankins is the senior ambassador in the program and is much beloved by the public. Michael McDuff has provided his fundraising talents to the team and has single-handedly raised the largest total contribution by any individual in the country for American Golf's Charity Foundation. At the foundation's dinner in 2015, Michael received the Unsung Hero Award for collecting donations on Tilden's seventh hole. He is no longer unsung!

CONCLUSION

When Tilden was built in 1936–37, there were only three other public eighteen-hole courses in all of Alameda and Contra Costa Counties.[126] Today, there are twenty-three. While closure or threat of closure looms large over many of the East Bay golf courses due to land use competition from real

Eighteenth (*left*) and fourteenth holes of Tilden Regional Park Golf Course. *Photo by the author.*

estate ventures and other pressures, Tilden is in a fortunate position since its land was secured by the regional park district eighty-three years ago. The stability enjoyed by the Tilden operation is the result of the determination of those who long ago imagined and provided for a beautiful recreational course to serve the public.

The golf course continues to be enjoyed by a wide variety of Bay Area golfers, young and old, walkers and riders, who can play a round at a reasonable cost in a reasonable amount of time, thanks to the cooperation of the public, supported by the course staff and the ambassadors. Play on!

7

CREATING LAKE ANZA

TILDEN AREA LANDMARKS

Wildcat Caves

Another landmark Tilden Park site owned by the Curran family was the famous Wildcat Caves. They are described by columnist Jack Burroughs in a 1957 story:

> *Huck Finn Apartments—before things like wall-to-wall rugs, window boxes and electrified kitchens existed. It had no central heating, no radiator pipes to pound with a poker on cold nights to rouse the janitor—even if there would be janitor to heave a grudging shovel full of coal into a non-existent basement furnace. Some part-time archeologists suspect it was used at some remote period as a snuggery by Indians who once inhabited this region.*

In modern times, according to James Curran, many University of California fraternity men received their initiation here.[127]

Known today as the Tilden Park Caves, they can be seen only from a distance, by hiking from Meadows Field along the Wildcat Gorge Trail and looking just below the Tilden merry-go-round. The caves are no longer accessible for liability reasons but are a reminder of the area's primitive volcanic history.

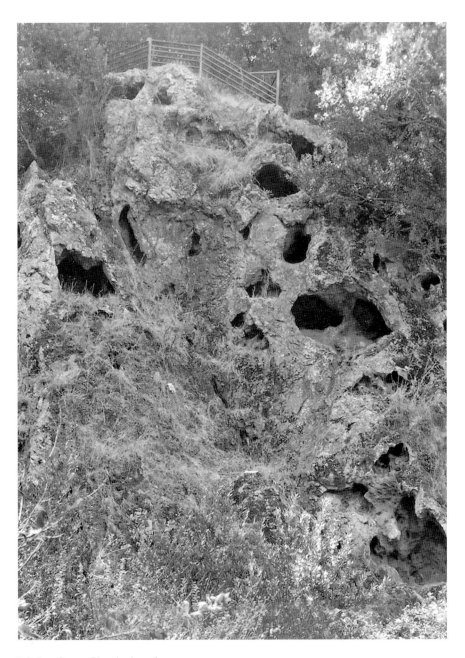

Wildcat Caves. *Photo by the author.*

Curran Farmhouse

Patrick and Mary Curran, natives of Montreal, Canada, came to California in the 1880s and purchased 318 acres from the Brissac family. Patrick and his ten children ran herds of cattle over the Berkeley Hills until 1909, when the Peoples Water Company secured the greater part of their holding by condemnation proceedings for watershed purposes.[128] According to James Curran in a 1949 interview, he and his sister Sarah were the last of the Wildcat Canyon farmers. They had a herd of cows and sold milk and butter in Berkeley until 1915.[129] The Currans had a fruit orchard in back of their farmhouse with about sixty apple, pear and cherry trees that the children loved to climb. The Curran farmhouse was located where the Orchard picnic area is now situated, just north of Lake Anza.

Curran farmhouse. On the bench are Mary Curran and her mother. *Photo by L.L. Stein; courtesy of EBRPD archives.*

Waterfalls and Streams

Prior to the creation of Lake Anza in 1938–39, the unfettered waters of Wildcat Creek were known by generations of Berkeley children who would roam around Wildcat Canyon and play in its creek and by its beautiful waterfall. The downside of the development of Lake Anza was the elimination of the canyon's largest waterfall.

Wildcat Creek waterfall, 1912. *Photo by C.W. Puhlmann; courtesy of EBRPD archives.*

WPA ENGINEERS DEVELOP PLAN FOR LAKE

As planning for the park's golf course progressed, WPA chief engineer E.E. Pixley stated in an April 1936 memo that building a dam would provide an inexpensive source of water for the soon-to-be-built course, but he wasn't sure if the resulting lake site would be suitable for its intended purpose. His concern was that "faults that had developed and the normal run-off of this area left it vulnerable to water loss through subterranean wastage," and he ordered test borings. Before any of this could be accomplished, the project was put on hold, as the limited WPA labor was focused on completing the golf course and tree planting.

In 1937, D.W. Albert, a widely known Berkeley engineer who had built the San Leandro and San Pablo dams, was retained to complete test borings; he subsequently pronounced the situation for the dam as "most ideal." The WPA plan called for the new lake to contain 150 million gallons over an eight-acre site set aside for this purpose. This new lake would be the second freshwater swimming pool open to the public in the Regional Park—the other being Lake Temescal.

In 1938, the WPA deferred the project, and General Manager Vail sent a new $100,000 grant request to the Public Works Administration. The grant was authorized within six weeks, on July 8, 1938. On August 25, a contract was awarded to private contractor Guerin Brothers for the construction of the concrete dam with an earth fill. Its dimensions: 240 feet in length and 15 feet in width at the top and 385 feet in width at the bottom. The spillway is 70 feet high. Total cost of the project when completed was $72,000, with the PWA funding $45,000 and the park district funding the balance.

Eight-acre site for new lake in process of being leveled. *Courtesy of EBRPD archives.*

Lake Anza, 1940. *Courtesy of EBRPD archives.*

IRRIGATION FOR GOLF COURSE

The original PWA grant for the construction of the Lake Anza dam was authorized as an irrigation project. It served that purpose and was also used as the source of water for the nearby golf course, thereby reducing the cost of operating the course. In a November 6, 1939 editorial, Superintendent Richard Walpole stated that the monthly EBMUD water bill was as much as $2,800 a month, so the substitution of lake water would quickly offset the lake's construction costs. "Pumped from the lake to a reservoir 1,500 feet higher in the hills, the water is then released—350,000 gallons per day—to keep up the golf course."[130] This water source was eventually eliminated because the lake water was only available intermittently; in dry years, there wasn't enough water to maintain the lake for both public swimming and for the golf course. Since 1965, the golf course has reverted to EBMUD as its sole source of irrigation water.

Aerial view showing the proximity of the golf course (*left*) to Lake Anza (*right*). *Courtesy of EBRPD archives.*

OPENING CEREMONIES

Lake Anza was opened on Sunday, May 7, 1939, with a crowd of about ten thousand, following a flag-raising ceremony. Activities included a luncheon put on by the Berkeley service clubs, an aquatic sports festival with diving and swimming races, an archery contest and a cricket match.

The Lake Anza name was chosen the day before the opening ceremony in a competition of East Bay children. School superintendents from Alameda and Contra Costa Counties were the judges, and the winner was twelve-year-old Margaret Magnussen, an eighth-grade student at Willard Junior High in Berkeley. She was awarded a twenty-five-dollar prize for submitting the winning name. Captain Juan Bautista de Anza was the leader of the Spanish expedition of 1776 that explored the East Bay area.[131]

Flag-raising ceremony. Pictured here are Josephine Abercrombie, who sang "My Country 'Tis of Thee," and Berkeley civic leader and future park director Emery Stone. *Courtesy of EBRPD archives.*

NEW BUILDING

WPA workmen built a clubhouse on the west shore of Lake Anza for $8,000. The structure, completed in March 1940, included a locker room, a boat, a bathhouse and accommodations for a caretaker.

SWIMMING PARADISE

1940

The opening day of swimming featured another elaborate aquatic sports carnival performance, this time with three stars of the Billy Rose Aquacade at the nearby Golden Gate International Exposition at Treasure Island. In addition to a diving exhibition, there were swimming races, canoe races and canoe-tilting contests as well as lifesaving demonstrations.

1942

The featured story in the September 17, 1942 *Oakland Tribune* was about eighteen-year-old Cisca Klein, from Holland, who had become the first female lifeguard at Lake Anza. Klein was a recent graduate of Berkeley High School and planned on registering at the University of California the following month. She was cited as an example of women's ability to fill positions vacated by men called to service or to the defense industry. Her father was himself in the shipbuilding industry. The Klein family had left Amsterdam three months before Hitler's armies invaded Holland.

1947

Four of the seven lifeguards on duty were UC students, all holders of senior Red Cross lifesaving certificates.[132]

1950s

Dale Roe supervised the lifeguards at Lake Anza and Lake Temescal; his year-round training program was said to have been a model all over Northern California. He organized annual water safety shows at the beginning of each season, alternating between Lake Temescal and Lake Anza. The shows were intended to save lives through education and entertainment.[133]

1960s

During the antiwar years, Lake Anza was an easy target. In 1962, vandals dynamited the dam, lowering the lake by about three feet. The following year, the stone boathouse built by the WPA was destroyed by a fire. The building, containing the caretaker's quarters, the dressing rooms and refreshment stands, was completely consumed in the blaze, causing $50,000 to $60,000 worth of damage and closing the lake for two years. The burnt structures were replaced, the lake was drained and improved and the beach was expanded to ten times its former size.

1970s

The "Age of Aquarius" continued into the '70s in Berkeley. Lake Anza had a reputation for nude bathing. It was reported that an X-rated movie called *Sip of Wine* had been filmed there, and the park board responded by passing Ordinance 38, prohibiting nude bathing within the parks.

FISHING PARADISE

In 1941, Lake Anza fish became the star attraction. The lake was stocked with adult fish: one hundred largemouth black bass, five hundred bluegills and twenty-eight green sunfish. This wasn't considered a lot of fish, and a limit of two black bass and three bluegills allowed per day was enforced on anglers. Efforts have been made every year since then to continue to supply the lake with sufficient fish to keep up with demand.

TODAY

Lake Anza is one of thirteen sites in the East Bay Regional Park District available for swimming and one of eleven sites available for fishing. Diving, which was popular in early years, has since been eliminated for liability reasons. Water quality is tested weekly between April and October when the lake is open. The population using the park's recreation facilities continues to grow, but the pressure has been reduced on the two original swim sites with the addition of seven swim lakes and beaches at new district parks. While usage is still high in the peak summer months, it is nothing like it was in the 1940s through the 1960s, when as many as 500,000 recreationalists flooded the parking lots around Lake Anza. Recent attendance averages:

Years	Attendance[134]
1997–1999	66,000
2000–2009	48,000
2010–2014	38,000
2015–2017	43,000

8

THE BRAZILIAN ROOM

The Brazilian Room is one of the most popular and highly utilized facilities in Tilden Park. It was constructed on a site that had previously been occupied by Peter Bruno, a native of Genoa, Italy, who came to the Bay Area in 1896. Bruno, a pioneer rancher, worked as a "water company guardian" while raising his children. He held a lease on ten thousand acres of land where he raised cattle in a broad area that eventually became parts of Orinda, Tilden Park, Wildcat Canyon and the town of San Pablo. Bruno retired in 1962 and moved to Lafayette, where he resided until his death in 1970 at the age of ninety-nine.[135]

GOLDEN GATE INTERNATIONAL EXPOSITION

The 1,728-square-foot ballroom with adjoining 1,896-square-foot patio, located at the center of Tilden Park, owes its name to an act of generosity by the country of Brazil. Brazil was one of the many nations that took part in the Golden Gate International Exposition, a two-year world's fair (1939–40) that drew seventeen million visitors from around the world. The art deco theme was "Pageant of the Pacific," showcasing the goods of nations sharing a border with the Pacific Ocean. "This was the first World's Fair to look beyond Europe for its inspiration."[136] The fair also celebrated the recent opening of the Bay Area's two new bridges, the San Francisco–Oakland

Peter Bruno raised his family on a cattle ranch on the site of the Brazilian Room. *Courtesy of EBRPD archives.*

Brazil Pavilion at 1939–40
World's Fair on Treasure Island.
Courtesy of EBRPD archives.

Bay Bridge in 1936 and the Golden Gate Bridge in 1937, and emphasized through this fair that the western United States was open to commerce with all the nations of the world.

The exposition had as its unusual site Treasure Island, the largest man-made island in history up until that time. The four-hundred-acre site was built with twenty million cubic yards of sand dredged from the bottom of San Francisco Bay by the U.S. Army Corps of Engineers between 1936 and 1937 for the exposition. It was just to the north of Yerba Buena Island, then occupied by the U.S. Navy. Both islands were connected to the Bay Bridge by means of a nine-hundred-foot causeway.[137]

Gardiner Dailey, the successful Bay Area architect of many upscale homes, designed the Brazil Pavilion at the exposition. The pavilion featured large interior and exterior murals, a big relief map of South America and oil paintings by noted Brazilian artists that hung above cases of semiprecious stones. An entire wing and garden were devoted to Café Brazil, which served Brazil's famous coffees. A South American orchestra entertained visitors.

Elbert Vail, park district manager, solicited various exhibitors for materials that would otherwise be discarded after the fair came to a close on September 29, 1940. Brazil responded to his solicitation and offered the district the materials that had been used in constructing the pavilion and exhibits. These included the pavilion's parquet floors, jacaranda wood walls, paneling and huge plate-glass mirrors.

TRANSFER OF BRAZIL PAVILION MATERIALS

Construction took about nine months. As planned, the recently built administration building was turned into a residential annex that was subsequently used by Richard Walpole as his family's home for more than a decade. The new ballroom opened onto a new wide patio. Regional park crews, with the assistance of the WPA, brought rock and stone from the vicinity of the North Gate, where the merry-go-round now stands, for the exterior of the new building.[138]

Park employees among PWA workers: Wes Adams (*top left*), Richard Walpole (*top right*), Georgette Morton and Austin "Buck" Dunn (*center*). The man in the vest is Elbert Vail. *Courtesy of EBRPD archives.*

OPENING CEREMONIES

On May 19, 1941, the *Oakland Tribune* announced: "Brazilian Room, Gift from Treasure Island Opened and Dedicated in Tilden Park." The next day, more than 1,500 visitors—including civic leaders, county and city officials and members of the social sets of Berkeley, Oakland and nearby East Bay cities—attended presentation ceremonies. Brazil's consul general, Anibal de Saboia Lima, gave the dedication: "This gift typifies the friendly relations between the two sister republics—the United States of America and the United States of Brazil." Acknowledging Brazil's gift of important materials, Major Tilden envisioned that "the Brazilian Room will be one of the places of entertainment for the soldiers and sailors and all citizens of the East Bay region."

Opening event at Brazilian Room, May 18, 1941. *Courtesy of EBRPD archives.*

Following the special program featuring Brazilian coffee, cookies and ice cream, the guests toured the grounds surrounding the new stone building. The landscaping resembled the original setting of the Brazil Pavilion on Treasure Island.[139]

SOLDIERS' RECREATIONAL FACILITY

With the completion of the Brazilian Room, recreational plans for the military moved along quickly. Vail announced that the first contingent of soldiers, from Fort Ord in the Monterey area, would enter Tilden Park two days later to enjoy a week of rest and relaxation. East Bay communities formed committees to organize lunches, teas and banquets and host games and dances to provide further entertainment for the soldiers. These activities gave the soldiers opportunities to mingle with women in safe and proper settings. The regional park, claimed Vail, would continue to provide for the recreational needs of these soldiers to relieve the monotony of drill and camp living.[140]

MUSIC CONCERTS

Beginning in 1941, the Brazilian Room hosted free public concerts on Sundays and holidays on its front lawn. Design engineer Howard W. Lindsay voluntarily organized these concerts and provided the broadcast technology. He placed two large speakers on the roof of the building and set out several smaller speakers on the lawn to play marches, light opera, popular melodies and classical music. Lindsay's free concerts continued throughout the war years and into 1946. By 1947, with the economy booming again, the concerts had resumed but were no longer free. Tickets were sold for $25 per concert or $500 for twenty concerts. Lindsay provided this program through 1950.[141]

Music played through speakers mounted on the roof of the Brazilian Room. *Courtesy of EBRPD archives.*

TODAY

The Brazilian Room underwent major seismic retrofitting in the 1970s in order to prepare the structure to withstand the region's inevitable earthquakes, due to its proximity to the Hayward Fault. The ballroom is still one of the premier wedding venues in the East Bay and is used for a wide range of events. Reservations for rental of the facility are usually made at least a year in advance.[142] Over recent years, the facility has averaged 243 events annually, with weddings accounting for 185 of these events, or 76 percent of the total.[143]

Brazilian Room used as a wedding venue in December 2018. *Courtesy of photographer Jenny Dee.*

9

THE REGIONAL PARK
BOTANIC GARDEN

As early as 1935, the U.S. Forest Service (USFS) research branch at the California Forest and Range Experiment Station in Berkeley was collecting California native plants. The work began with seed-germination research and later dealt with erosion control on mountain roads and the landscaping of USFS grounds throughout California. In Tilden, the USFS involved the CCC in the collection of seeds. Soon there was a large and varied repository of native trees and shrubs at the Berkeley station.

FATHER OF THE BOTANIC GARDEN

In February 1938, Howard McMinn, professor of botany at Mills College, joined the EBRPD board as a temporary replacement for Dr. Reinhardt.[144] A frequent visitor to the California Forest and Range Experimental Service nursery, also known as the Gill Nursery, in West Berkeley, McMinn had seen its plant collection and realized the potential. He thought it could form the basis for a native plant botanic garden and persuaded the park district to enter a cooperative agreement with the USFS. If the USFS provided the plants, the district would provide the land to create the garden. For taking this initiative, McMinn is

Howard McMinn, professor of botany. *Courtesy of EBRPD archives.*

considered the "father of the Botanic Garden." August Vollmer, in his last years on the board, also played a huge role in shepherding the garden through its early difficulties and aiding its progress in every possible way.[145]

JAMES ROOF, FIRST DIRECTOR

The park district recognized the need to hire a manager to oversee the development of the garden. They found their man in Jim Roof. Roof had joined the USFS, in 1935, assigned to the Berkeley station. By 1937, he had become the nursery superintendent. In 1939, McMinn wanted him transferred to the EBRPD to start the new botanic garden in Tilden Park and become its first director, but Roof had no desire to leave the USFS. Finally, the parties reached an agreement; Roof would work half-time for the service and half-time for the park district.

McMinn assembled a special committee, including August Vollmer from the park district and representatives from the U.S. Forest Service, the University of California, the Sierra Club and others, to select a site for the garden. The members chose the site of Pascuale Bruno's ranch, the same location of the

Director Jim Roof in the Botanic Garden, May 24, 1949. *Courtesy of EBRPD archives.*

Botanic Garden today. Bruno had been a caretaker for the East Bay Water Company in upper Wildcat Canyon in the 1920s. The location is ideally situated between interior heat and mild coastal influences, allowing cultivation of the broadest possible variety of California native plants.[146]

Roof started construction at the Botanic Garden on January 1, 1940. In May, the now celebrated Mountain Meadow was graded, sodded and planted with lodgepole pines, white firs and quaking aspens. Work proceeded rapidly; there were hundreds of WPA men in Tilden Park, and they were on call for work in the garden whenever needed. For one critical stretch, Roof had three hundred men working in the garden for several months.

TREE PLANTING

John McLaren, the famous landscape designer of Golden Gate Park, was appointed by the EBRPD to provide design consultation for tree planting within the park district. Starting in 1938, the first two thousand redwood trees arrived by ship from the Union Lumber Company at Fort Bragg.[147] From 1940 to 1941, more than fifty-seven thousand plants from the USFS nursery and an additional forty-two thousand plants from Tilden Park nurseries were used on the Tilden Park golf course and adjacent parklands, including Jewel Lake and Lake Anza, as well as Lake Temescal and Redwood Regional Parks. All this was done by WPA crews under Roof's direction while he continued to supervise development of the Botanic Garden.

WAR YEARS

From 1939 to 1941, just prior to the United States' involvement in World War II, Roof continued his work with the regional parks while acting as consultant with the U.S. Army regarding the use of plants to conceal the fortifications and big guns of Fort Barry and Fort Cronkite on the Marin coast. Then, in 1942, Roof was drafted. Steve Edwards, the third director of the Botanic Garden, described what happened:

> *Jim was drafted and sent to Camp Roberts near San Luis Obispo, where he was readied to fight in the Pacific. Roof's fellow soldiers went to New*

Guinea to meet the Japanese who were attacking Port Darwin, producing some of the bloodiest fighting of the war. At the last minute an order had been sent in Roof's behalf by someone who knew his horticultural expertise, and he was sent to England to serve in the camouflage corps. We all know what vital work that was for the liberation of France, but Roof's role was special. He was a strikingly handsome man, and, according to Walter Knight, Jim looked sufficiently like General Eisenhower that he was used as a double at parades and other events that Ike did not care to attend.[148]

POSTWAR PERIOD

When Roof returned to work in February 1946, the garden had become a coastal jungle; there had been no one to care for the young Botanic Garden. Richard Walpole, appointed superintendent of Tilden Park in 1942 and general manager of the park district in 1945, could only send a watering man once or twice a week to turn on the garden's watering system to keep the plants alive. Tall weeds and poison oak were everywhere. The grass in

Ferndale section of the garden, 1942. *Photo by A.E. Wieslander; courtesy of EBRPD archives.*

the meadows was three feet high, and the creek was a jungle of willows. There were no longer any WPA crews to clean up the mess. Roof started the cleanup alone and then hired an assistant, Robert Owen, in 1947. Owen stayed with him until 1962. Owen taught high school classes in landscape gardening and provided guided tours of the Tilden's botanic offerings in addition to other duties at the garden. From 1948 on, they had only a few assistants of high school and college age who received little pay but wonderful botanical training.

> *By 1952 the garden was well enough under control that Roof and Owen began to take regular field-collecting trips around the state in order to expand their collection of native plants. This full-fledged botanical field collecting continued for 10 years during which time Roof and his crew visited the Sierra Nevada, Death Valley, Lassen to the Monterey Peninsula, San Diego County and the Mexican border to the Marble Mountains Wilderness area. Roof's native collection burgeoned to become one of the most comprehensive in the country.*[149]

"ROOF" STORIES

One description of Roof suggests that his whole life and energy seemed channeled into collecting and planting, as he felt a closer kinship to trees than to people. Born in a refugee's shack four years after the 1906 San Francisco earthquake, Roof grew up in the southwest part of San Francisco, which was mostly open country at the time. From an early age, Roof was aware of the native plants that grew near his home, and he reveled in the fields of spring flowers that grew where he played around Lake Merced. He took an interest in learning the names of trees and shrubs around age twelve while on a family trip to the Rockies. Barely into his teens, Roof and his friends often played hooky to hike on Mount Tamalpais. After high school, Jim joined a band of mountain dwellers on Tamalpais to live off the land during hard times. When he joined the USFS at age twenty-five, it was the fulfillment of a dream.[150]

> *In the late 1960s and into the 1970s Jim lived, with his large collection of jazz records, in an old WPA-built stone restroom, that he converted into a domicile, at Mineral Springs between Inspiration Pointe and the garden.*

Annoyed by people banging on his door at all hours of the night, he hammered four-inch nails through the thick wooden door so a "bed" of their sharp points protruded well to the outside. If you've ever seen a picture of a yogi lying on a bed of nails, you'll know what the door was like. I saw it and touched it.[151]

One of Steve Edwards's most cherished memories of Jim is of his *whistling*, something he tended to do while watering plant beds. Edwards said that "crooner Bing Crosby was famous for his whistling, but didn't hold a candle to Jim. Jim's whistle was far more powerful by far, easily enjoyed halfway across the garden, and melodious as meadowlarks. I've never since heard anyone whistle like that. It told of his contentment doing work he was born to do, in a garden of his own creation."[152]

Edwards still considers the garden "haunted by the powerful presence of Jim Roof, curiously the garden's strongest guarantor of tranquility."

He realized that people needed refuge from society's supposed progress as thousands of half-stunned visitors came to the garden every year seeking refuge. The character of this garden was forged in the furnace of Jim Roof's love for a California of old, in all its irresistible simplicity. Strolling through the garden a quiet evening, his haunting presence can be a thing of joy.[153]

ROOF CONTROVERSY

During the mid-1960s, the Tilden Regional Botanic Garden was at the center of two interwoven controversies: one related to a long range plan for the garden, the other to the status of Director Roof.

FRIENDS OF THE BOTANIC GARDEN

December 4, 1962, was the first meeting of a group of "garden regulars" who were concerned about the sour relations between Jim Roof and the newly appointed district general manager, William Penn Mott, as well as the lack of financial support for the Botanic Garden. In response, the group formed a new organization, Friends of the Botanic Garden, to develop a plan for saving the garden.

The chairman of the organization was Jim Roof's ally and mentor Rimo Bacigalupi, manager of the UC Jepson Herbarium.[154] The Friends appointed four people to a planning subcommittee: Charles Kraebal and A.E. Weislander, both retired U.S. Forest Service members; Mai Arbegast of the UC landscaping department; and Chairman Owen Pearce, editor of various horticultural publications.[155]

Bacigalupi and his allies advocated expanding Tilden's six-acre botanic garden and prepared detailed recommendations for its improvement. A small splinter Native Parks group led by Owen Pearce advocated retaining the garden and also establishing a four-hundred-acre ecological study Reserve in Anthony Chabot Regional Park, similar in concept to the Rancho Santa Ana Botanic Garden. Ironically, the two camps were headed by and included leading members from the state's prestigious Botanical and Horticultural Societies.

Specific details for the Friends and Native Park proposals became clear when Rimo Bacigalupi sent a letter to park board president Robert Gordon Sproul in June 1964 with tentative suggestions for both the existing six-acre garden and a proposed five-acre extension.

Mott and district staff had been involved in continuing disputes with Roof about operational, aesthetic and safety issues at the garden; this all came to a head in February 1965 while Mott was in Australia. Roof received his twenty-five-year service pin, followed ten days later by a letter of termination citing alleged insubordination.

A "Save the Garden" coordinating committee quickly organized to save both Roof and the Regional Park Botanic Garden. Lobbying at the district board level was intense, with active media attention focused on the regional park board's April 6 meeting. Some 3,200 signatures were collected by groups in favor of keeping the garden in Tilden. After hearing well-organized public comments, the board adopted a resolution clarifying its policy "to not destroy, remove, or diminish the size or quality of the existing California Native Plant Garden at Tilden," and stating that Roof would remain director, pending a hearing by Mott.

Mott scheduled a meeting on April 8, 1965, to review the circumstances that had prompted Roof's termination. EBRPD public relations chief Richard Trudeau and Alameda County district attorney Dick Moore testified that the charges in the letter of termination could not be sustained in the face of such strong public support for both Roof and the garden. Mott reluctantly reinstated Roof during his five-hour grievance hearing and developed guidelines for the staff to work with Roof to improve the garden.[156]

CALIFORNIA NATIVE PLANT SOCIETY

At a dinner after the April 8 showdown with the board, members of the original Friends created the California Native Plant Society (CNPS). Incorporation papers were filed on August 12, 1965, listing forty-five founding members. Watson M. Laetsch, a UC assistant professor of botany, was elected its first president. Jim Roof served as vice president on the statewide board of CNPS for several terms and then led the group as its director for many more years; he continued to serve as the group's horticultural advisor until his death in 1983.[157] CNPS has grown into a statewide organization of nearly ten thousand members in thirty-three regional chapters that promotes native plant appreciation, research, education and conservation through five statewide programs.[158]

CONTROVERSY'S CONCLUSION

On December 28, 1965, the report of the board's special committee on EBRPD Botanic Gardens was presented to the full board. The report included fourteen specific recommendations, beginning with upgrading a garden master plan, creating a five-year financing and development plan and clarifying that the responsibility for planting and maintenance of the Regional Park Botanic Garden should be the sole responsibility of its director. Having served the intended purpose, the original Friends organization was disbanded until the 1990s, when it was resurrected as the Friends of the Regional Parks Botanic Garden under Steve Edwards.

JAMES B. ROOF VISITOR CENTER

In 1973, a small visitor center was built, with crew offices, a reception room and an auditorium. The long-needed 1,600-square-foot, $65,000 building was constructed at the entrance to the Botanic Garden. It was designed by architect Don Harms, assistant chief of the EBRPD Design and Construction Department. The architecture is described as "Bay Area Rustic."[159]

ROOF'S RETIREMENT AND SEARCH
FOR HIS SUCCESSOR

Although Roof turned sixty-five, the mandatory age of retirement, in September 1975, he was permitted to continue his employment at the Botanic Garden for another year while the board searched for his replacement. Dr. Brewer asked park directors to find the best qualified successor who might be able to gain from Roof's knowledge and experience. Dr. Brewer offered his own assistance, along with five other botanical experts; their help was gratefully accepted.[160] Finally, in August 1976, Wayne Roderick was chosen as Roof's successor. Roof passed away seven years later.

WAYNE RODERICK, SECOND DIRECTOR

In a 2004 *Manzanita* article titled "The Excellent Director," Steve Edwards notes that Roderick was practically everyone's first choice. He had already earned a reputation for transforming the native area of the University of California's Botanic Garden over a twenty-four-year period. Before that, he had owned an ornamental plant nursery with his father for fifteen years in Petaluma. According to Edwards, the selection of Roderick was "one of the great decisions in the truly remarkable history of the East Bay Regional Park District."

Roderick served a relatively short tenure, between 1976 and 1983, but had a significant influence on those he managed, as Edwards recalled:

> We lived in awe of *Jim Roof*; we were inspired by him and learned a huge amount from him. With Wayne, we learned at an even faster rate, for he made it a critical part of his job to cultivate the garden crew: he trained us, gave us opportunities, and was always there for us.
>
> Park district management asked Wayne to get public programs up and running in the Visitor Center. He started a lecture series from scratch, sometimes speaking to only two or three people at a time, and gradually built it up into something to be proud of. That's why, after his retirement, we named the Saturday morning lecture series after him—The Wayne Roderick Lectures. Wayne vastly improved the garden collections, created our first major volunteer program, integrated the Garden into the Park District, made the place a fully public garden, then proceeded to put it on

Wayne Roderick, second director. *Courtesy of EBRPD archives.*

the map internationally. Best of all, he attracted many of the people who became our most constant supporters, volunteers, and cherished members of our garden community.[161]

STEVE EDWARDS, THIRD DIRECTOR

Edwards's career was shaped by his interactions with the garden's first two directors while he was a student. He embraced the mission of the garden and contributed to the garden publications. In an article for *Pacific Horticulture* shortly before his retirement, he shared his thoughts about his career:

A young gangly Saint Mary's College student walked into the Botanic Garden in 1969 to apply for a summer job. He approached a weather-beaten old man working in the garden and asked for Jim Roof. Not looking up, the man's instant response was "Gone to Alaska—on vacation."

Undeterred, the college student pressed on. The old man removed his hat, tossed it over a nearby plant label and asked: "What's the name of this tree?" The kid straightened up and quickly provided a species of pine very close to the correct answer. "Not bad, not bad at all," said the old man, who in fact was the prankster Roof himself. Thus began the 43-year career with the Botanic Garden of Stephen W. Edwards.

Edwards graduated summa cum laude *in 1973 from Saint Mary's College of Moraga, California, with a B.A. in Philosophy; he earned his Master's Degree in Paleontology in 1975 from UC Berkeley. In 1983 he received his PhD in paleobotany. Edwards worked for Roof for a couple of years during the summer when he was still attending Saint Mary's. He followed Roof's foreman to Las Trampas Regional Wilderness near Danville where he worked for six years while continuing his studies at UC ("Paleontologists take a long time to graduate").*

Edwards returned to the Botanic Garden in 1978 after Roof retired and Roderick became director. According to Edwards, Roderick "treated his employees like gold." When Roderick retired, Edwards became the third director in a 31-year period to hold that position.

Edwards and Roderick characterized one important function of the Garden as "an ark" that temporarily held threatened plants. Their work focused on propagating and increasing these plants, and then reintroducing them when safe havens could be secured in their natural wild.

Steve Edwards, third director.
Photo by the author.

Under the Director's stewardship, the garden has done exactly what garden preservation is designed to do: protect the wild. The first of these re-introductions was in 1966, when seed from the Antioch primrose—collected and protected at the Botanic Garden—was eventually sowed on Brannon Island and later on Brown's Island in the Sacramento River Delta. More recently, several plants which had been collected by Botanic Garden staff from San Bruno Mountain were saved because they had become completely extinct in the wild; in cooperation with San Mateo County park staff, these species were reintroduced. [162]

THE GARDEN'S FOURFOLD MISSION

As described by Edwards, the Botanic Garden and other similar preserves share a fourfold mission in how they serve both the public and nature:

1. EXHIBITIONS. The park should create and maintain a diverse and beautiful garden for public enjoyment, using only California native plants.

2. CONSERVATION. The Botanic Garden is to protect rare and endangered species, which account for between 10 and 15 percent of the species in the garden.

3. RESEARCH. The park provides a place for horticultural experimentation, field collection and documentation as well as provides a workshop for selecting new "cultivars" that can be introduced into public and private gardens.[163]

4. EDUCATION. Glenn Keator has led an excellent thirteen-to-sixteen-week docent program for the last ten years that included annual docent enrichment field trips. Through publications, the public is informed about the garden's projects and activities. The Botanic Garden produces *The Four Seasons, Journal of the Botanic Garden*, an annual journal, and *Manzanita*, a quarterly newsletter. The garden also maintains a comprehensive website that includes a list of classes and events, a seasonal guide and photographs. It is available at nativeplants.org.

EXHIBITIONS

The ten-acre garden is divided in ten sections, each representing a different aspect of California's biological diversity. Edwards cited his specific contributions to three areas of the exhibition:

NATIVE GRASSES—"I've added an amazing collection of native perennial grasses."

ROCK GARDEN—"Roderick started it at the end of his career, and I've enlarged it."

EXPANSION—"The garden has been enlarged in my time from seven to ten acres."

CONSERVATION

Edwards is proud of the garden's rare plant collection: "A lot of what you see here at the garden is endangered. That will always be one of our foci."

RESEARCH

Edwards cited the research contributions of two supervisors under his administration, Al Seneras and Joe Dahl.

EDUCATION

Edwards described the creation of the Friends of the Botanic Garden, including the growth of its docent program, as his contribution to the education program. Docents are available to the public for free tours. From November through February, the Botanic Garden hosts the Wayne Roderick Winter Lecture Series.

One of the things that Edwards was very proud of was his development of the garden's publication, *Four Seasons*. This journal of the Botanic Garden is published annually. It is sent out to all the best horticultural libraries. "It's a benefit to membership, but I've turned it into a really great journal."

EDWARDS'S FINAL MESSAGE

When Edwards retired at the end of 2013, the final message he left on his computer to his staff spoke volumes: "Bless you all. I never expected to love you all so much. That could change fast if you don't water the plants! Steve."

BART O'BRIEN, FOURTH DIRECTOR

The transition from Steve Edwards to his successor was well planned. Bart O'Brien has a degree in environmental planning and management from UC Davis as well as a master's in landscape architecture from Harvard University. He has considered Edwards a valuable friend and colleague since the 1980s; he had worked at Yerba Buena Nursery in Half Moon Bay and visited the Regional Park's Botanic Garden regularly. Previously, O'Brien served as director of special projects for the Rancho Santa Ana Botanic Garden (RSABG) in Claremont, California.

Bart O'Brien, current director. *Photo by the author.*

O'Brien said, "I was quite surprised when Edwards called to tell me of his plan to retire....I would never have thought that I would have the opportunity to lead this extraordinary garden, the only place that could (and did!) tempt me away from my work at Rancho Santa Ana Garden (RSABG)."[164] RSABG, about thirty-five miles east of Los Angeles in the foothills of the San Gabriel Mountains, is the largest botanical garden dedicated to California native plants, with over two thousand taxa (types) of California plants spread across eighty-six acres. Although Tilden, at only ten acres, is much smaller, it is unique for its sloping site and for its microclimates, which enable the widest range of native California plants anywhere in the country.

During his career in conservation, O'Brien participated in planning, restoration and landscape projects for the Los Angeles and San Gabriel Rivers and watersheds in Southern California. He held leadership roles in the California Native Plant Society (CNPS) and is both the state archivist for the organization and a member of its editorial board for the journal *Fremontia*. He has authored numerous articles, presented lectures and symposia and developed and managed a new native plant horticulture education and outreach program for RSABG.

O'Brien made several remarkable contributions to the park in three main areas that fulfill the garden's core mission: native plant horticulture, conservation and education. Among his future goals are designing and developing an expanded visitor center and parking lot north of the current Botanic Garden site. He would like to expand public programs such as the annual fall sale on the first Saturday of October, cosponsored by the CNPS.

Like his predecessors, O'Brien's main focus is plant conservation, especially as weather extremes caused by climate change bring urgency to the need for preservation of California native species. O'Brien is continuing the program of sending all types of collected California plant life to special preservation centers with liquid nitrogen freezers. Tilden Botanic Garden has already been successful in several instances of restoring plant species that would have otherwise become extinct.

NATIVE HERE NURSERY

The Native Here Nursery, located at 101 Golf Course Drive in Berkeley, is exactly one mile from the Botanic Garden. The nursery is situated opposite the entrance to the Tilden Park golf course. On January 1, 1994, after two years of negotiation over possible locations, the park district entered into a special-use agreement with the Native Here Nursery, a project of the East Bay Chapter of the California Native Plant Society.

The purpose of this nonprofit nursery is to contribute to the preservation of California native flora by growing and selling plants for private gardening projects. These "locally native" plants are grown from seed and cuttings collected in Alameda and Contra Costa Counties. The nursery's mission includes educating the public about native plants and providing native plants for the public, nurseries, contractors and environmental consultants. The website www.nativeherenursery.org provides hours of operation, plant inventories and images, a newsletter and a description of volunteer opportunities.

Native Here Nursery sign. *Photo by the author.*

10

HISTORY OF MILITARY IN TILDEN PARK

B etween 1941 and 1973, the U.S. Army leased three separate sites in Tilden Park for military purposes; one was well publicized, while two others were kept secret until after the leases were abandoned.

At the onset of World War II, the park board immediately recognized its new responsibility to offer opportunities for recreation and rest to armed forces personnel who were stationed in the Bay Area, to offset their homesickness and the monotony of life in military camps. Several board members and staff had served as officers in the First World War and felt their obligation firsthand to the servicemen and to the Roosevelt administration that had so recently provided the funds and manpower for developing the parks. Now it was time to give back.

WILDCAT CANYON ARMY CAMP: SITE 1

The first of the three Tilden Park sites used by the army was Camp Wildcat Canyon, in the northwest section of the park. The U.S. Army had leased the Wildcat Canyon camp site since 1934, while operating the CCC camp in cooperation with the National Park Service (see chapter 4). In April 1941, after transporting away the last contingent of CCC boys, the army prepared the camp for its next mission: to provide training, recreation and recuperation to service personnel.[165]

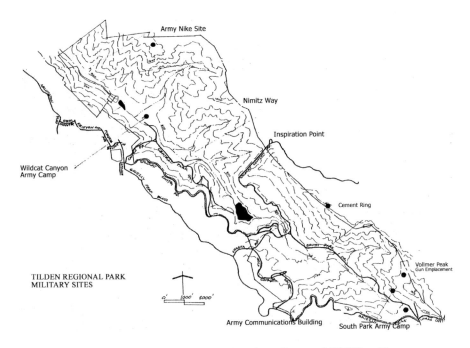

Map of Tilden Park and former military site locations. *Courtesy of EBRPD archives.*

Soldiers playing baseball on Meadows Field near Camp Wildcat Canyon. *Courtesy of EBRPD archives.*

RECREATION CENTER

The first contingent of five hundred soldiers from the Seventh Infantry Division's training facility at Monterey's Fort Ord arrived on May 20 for the first of a series of weeklong encampments. Recreational activities afforded the troops within Tilden Park included swimming, golfing and hiking on its newly created trails. The Brazilian Room facilities were also made available for parties, and its lawn was often used for softball games. The Berkeley community also went out of its way to welcome the soldiers to the area by providing free access to its entertainment facilities, including the ice rink, motion picture houses and the Greek Theater for university-sponsored events, including dances.

CONVALESCENT HOSPITAL

Camp Wildcat Canyon was reopened in 1944 by the Oakland Regional Hospital as an "occupational therapy laboratory and reconditioning annex" for soldiers recuperating from their military service. The camp proved a success, as patients made the camp their own by painting, weeding, cutting wood or using a machine shop to perform tasks such as fixing jeeps on weekdays. They made use of the nearby recreational facilities on weekends.[166]

ANTIAIRCRAFT BATTERIES AND TRAINING CENTER

During World War II, two thousand soldiers were stationed throughout Tilden Park, manning antiaircraft batteries in the northern and southern ends of the park. The antiaircraft battery in the Nature Area was hidden in a thick eucalyptus grove. This area was also used as a training facility, with a rifle range and level drilling ground established in 175 acres in Wildcat Canyon adjacent to the former CCC camp. Some of the soldiers guarded prisoners of war in a 200-square-foot stockade.[167]

SOUTH PARK ARMY CAMP: SITE 2

In February 1942, attacks by a Japanese submarine sank several merchant vessels and bombarded Ellwood Field near Santa Barbara, triggering the fear of a West Coast invasion. In June 1942, a small Japanese force occupied two small islands in the Aleutians in Alaska and remained there for over a year until a joint U.S./Canadian force ejected them.[168] The Japanese reasoned that control of the Aleutians would prevent a possible U.S. attack across the northern Pacific. Similarly, the United States feared that the islands would be used as bases from which to launch aerial assaults against the West Coast.

In 1942, the army leased a second site on the southern end of Tilden Park known as the South Park Army Camp. The camp would contain the radar control station and its supporting Vollmer Peak Gun Emplacement. It was not until August 28, 1945, that the existence of the army's radar center in Tilden Park was revealed to the public and dubbed the "Watchdog of the West Coast." A total of five hundred men occupied South Park Army Camp during wartime. The army continued to lease the site until November 1959.

RADAR CONTROL STATION

The secret four-story radar control station, with three stories underground, was moved from downtown Oakland on July 1, 1944. The elaborate facility, with four-foot-thick bomb- and gas-proof walls, was known as the "Salt Mine."[169] It was built to protect the West Coast from enemy attack by air or sea.

The Berkeley station was the nerve center for fifteen radar centers in Northern California and was responsible for guarding U.S. territory from the Oregon border in the north to San Luis Obispo, California, in the south and the entire state of Nevada to the east. The facility was manned by sixty men providing twenty-four-hour coverage to intercept enemy planes and direct antiaircraft fire and operations of fighter planes.[170]

VOLLMER PEAK ARTILLERY GUN EMPLACEMENT

Two hundred feet above the radar facility on Vollmer Peak, two artillery gun emplacements were manned around the clock. After V-J Day (August 14, 1945, marking the end of World War II), the radar station continued to be operated by the Fourth Army Air Force, concentrating on search and rescue operations.

The National Guard Antiaircraft Battery took over the defense operation in 1953.[171] According to Private First Class Leon McClung from Mableton, Georgia, who provided an account of his experiences manning the gun emplacement in 1953–54, "There were 90 MM gun emplacements called Battery B on Vollmer Peak that were manned by the 752 Artillery Anti-Aircraft unit (zone 8)." Seventeen permanent National Guard employees were assigned training and maintenance duties, while many guardsmen serving as "weekend warriors" were students at the University of California.[172]

Abandoned South Park Camp site after cancelation of army lease in 1959. *Courtesy of EBRPD archives.*

THE COLD WAR: NIKE MISSILE ERA

After the end of World War II, the U.S. military planners were concerned about Soviet Union bombers attacking undefended urban centers and military installations. To that end, by 1946, the United States had developed the Nike-Ajax missile, the nation's first supersonic antiaircraft guided missile. It was designed to intercept and destroy all types of bomber aircraft.

This placement of Nike missiles, launchers and attendant radars comprised a Nike missile battery or base. By 1953, the Nike bases, under the auspices of the U.S. Army, operated around vital industrial areas and densely populated strategic areas. Eleven Nike missile bases encircled the Bay Area. The first base was established in San Francisco in 1954. The bases were considered top secret and completely off-limits to the general public.[173]

NIKE MISSILE STATION: SITE 3

In 1959, the army purchased approximately 70 acres in Wildcat Canyon and 60 acres of EBMUD land adjoining Tilden Park to house a Nike missile installation consisting of twenty-four Nike-Ajax guided missiles. Maintenance and housing facilities for army personnel were located on 5,128 acres of land within Tilden's borders.[174] Today's popular Nimitz Way hiking trail was once the carefully guarded entrance to the installation complex.

A division of Bell Telephone designed and installed the Nike system.[175] Due to the technical requirements of the systems of those days, the radars used by Nike had to be located at least one mile away from the missile launchers and also had to have a clear line of sight to the missile from launch to detonation. The radars used in the Wildcat Canyon installation were located on Potrero Ridge about one and a half miles north and on Vollmer Peak one and a half miles south of the missile-launching site. Six radars were in use. In addition to the radar buildings and missile launch and storage facilities, each site had administration buildings, housing and training facilities. There was around-the-clock military presence with dozens of military personnel and guard dogs. In July 1958, the operation of the Bay Area's Nike bases was transferred from the U.S. Army to the National Guard.

Most of the Nike missile bases in the Bay Area had a brief life span; by 1962, they were already being deactivated. Changing military technology

Wildcat Canyon
Nike Missile Site.
*Courtesy of El
Cerrito Historical
Society.*

made attack from long-range bombers unlikely, and intercontinental ballistic missiles (ICBMs) were beginning to be deployed instead.

Between 1962 and 1973, the former Nike missile site was known as the haunted village, named in 1963 by "Lonesome" Bill Foley, the army private assigned to guard the village. There was no longer any water, electricity or sewer service, and the structures had been badly vandalized. The site was located three miles into the park from the entrance and required a lot of patrolling.[176]

Ellen Thomsen, owner of the Redwood Valley Railway concession, noted that in 1973, the railway was offered access to the materials from the village and used them in subsequent railway facility improvements. The terminus for the railroad is named Army Camp to reflect the site's military history.

Between 1941 and 1973, the EBRPD leased a portion of its land to the U.S. Army to support defensive operations that the government considered necessary in light of real or perceived threats. The fact that this duty was performed in secret allowed the park district to continue to perform its primary mission, to provide recreation to all the citizens of the East Bay.

CEMENT RING

Many have wondered about the purpose of the concrete ring located about a mile up the Sea View Trail south of Wildcat Canyon Road. Two EBRPD documents described its dual purpose.

Cement Ring. *Photo by the author.*

A Vail memo dated December 12, 1941, describes the structure as "The Mirador," a portion of the Brazilian Pavilion from the Golden Gate International Exposition being used as an army observation point.

A 1971 document states that a glass-walled rotunda used as a coffee room within the Brazilian Pavilion, where it served for many years as a comfortable and popular lookout point for visitors, had been dismantled by WPA crews.[177]

TWO MEMORIAL SITES DEDICATED

Nimitz Way

Nimitz Way was dedicated to Admiral Chester W. Nimitz on November 5, 1955. He was a Berkeley resident who played a major role in the naval history of World War II as the commander in chief of the U.S. Pacific Fleet and commander in chief of the Pacific for the U.S. and Allied air, land and sea forces during World War II.

Dedication of Nimitz Way. Admiral Nimitz in front of plaque, May 5, 1955. *Courtesy of EBRPD archives.*

On various occasions, EBRPD chairman Robert Sibley had met Admiral and Catherine Nimitz hiking in Tilden Park. Nimitz enjoyed hiking along the trail from Inspiration Point to Wildcat Peak and had sown yellow lupine seed along the trail to further enhance the scenery. Sibley suggested to the board that they consider naming the trail after Nimitz in light of his love of Tilden Park and his great stature as a citizen of the community.

The dedication ceremony was attended by a large crowd of people, followed by a tea at the Brazilian Room where Mrs. Nimitz's paintings of Jewel Lake and other areas in the park were on display.

Rotary Peace Grove

In 1955, Robert Sibley, a past president (1947–48) of the Berkeley Rotary Club, conceived the plan to establish a Rotary Peace Grove and every

Bill Mott (*left*) and
Adlai Stevenson at the
Rotary Peace Grove
in 1963. *Courtesy of
EBRPD archives.*

year honor a person who has contributed toward the Rotary principles of international understanding, goodwill and peace through world fellowship. The grove is within Tilden Park, adjacent to the former site of the Nike Missile Base.

In 1956, the first year, one hundred giant sequoia trees were planted in honor of Paul Harris, founder of Rotary International. Each year, a new plaque is added and a tree is planted for the honoree. In 1963, the recipient was Adlai Stevenson, U.S. ambassador to the United Nations, a childhood resident of Berkeley. Pope Francis was a recent recipient.[178]

PART III

POSTWAR YEARS:
NEW ATTRACTIONS

II

REMEMBERING RICHARD WALPOLE

Richard Walpole's career with the EBRPD spanned nearly a quarter century, from 1937 to 1960. Although for most of his tenure the system consisted of four parks—Tilden, Sibley, Temescal and Redwood—it was the development and maintenance of Tilden Park that required his greatest attention.[179] During his long career, Walpole lead the development (some say overdevelopment) of Tilden as it became the natural and recreational center for the entire East Bay.

Walpole was born in Memphis, Tennessee, on March 13, 1911. His parents were vaudeville performers billed as the LaGardos. The family act traveled the South's vaudeville circuit for years until vaudeville was replaced by the "moving pictures." The family moved to Oakland, California, where Richard attended elementary school, then settled in Southern California for most of his adolescence. Just days after his twentieth birthday, Walpole married Margaret M. Whidden on March 24, 1931. She had just turned sixteen.

Walpole began to work for the Los Angeles Parks Department in 1933 as an apprentice, serving both William Johnson, superintendent of the Griffith Park Golf Courses, and architect William P. "Billy" Bell. Bell was in the process of redesigning three of the Griffith Park courses between 1933 and 1937. Walpole was determined to impress Bell. He was put in charge of "redeveloping LA's Old Municipal Sand Memorial links into a modern all-grass nine-hole course" between October 1936 and June 1937. The nine-hole course was renamed the Roosevelt Municipal Course when it was finally completed in October 1937.[180]

Richard E. Walpole. *Courtesy of Mel Walpole Peters.*

ARRIVAL AT TILDEN PARK GOLF COURSE

In his diary, Walpole describes being brought to Northern California by Bell in June 1937 to manage the seeding of the Tilden Park golf course and other work to make the course operational. Billy Bell had designed the course in 1936, and WPA crews had already carved the course out of a dense eucalyptus grove. Walpole was repeatedly advised by Bell that this project might lead to something good. Walpole spent six twelve-hour days each week at the course and then drove home to take his wife out to a movie or stay home to read a library book, such as Dale Carnegie's *How to Win Friends and Influence People*.

Walpole's work ethic and charm must have been well received; at the end of the project, before his scheduled return to Los Angeles, the board appointed him superintendent and general manager of the Tilden course in 1938.

Walpole participated in an honorary capacity in the formation of the two-hundred-member Men's Club. He helped the service clubs organize tournaments and provided constant publicity for the course, including writing an entertaining weekly golf column in the *Berkeley Daily Gazette* called Along the Fairways.

The start of World War II shifted focus away from local recreation needs toward the national emergency. Locally, Elbert Vail resigned from the park district to take a position in the defense industry. The board selected his successor, Harold Curtiss, who assumed duty in May 1942. At the board's suggestion, Curtiss appointed Walpole as superintendent of Tilden Park, succeeding Mark Green, who had also left to do defense work. Walpole received a wartime draft exemption from Governor Earl Warren to head the East Bay Hills Fire Protective Association.

Walpole became president of the East Bay Regional Parks Employee Association and, on January 8, 1945, brought a resolution to the park board stating that the employees had unanimously voted to call for Harold Curtiss's resignation because of how he treated them. The resolution succeeded in getting Curtiss to resign, and Walpole then applied for the now vacant position. His name was brought before the five-member park board on March 25, 1945, and he was voted in by a three-to-two vote.

The early period of Walpole's tenure as regional park district manager coincided with the postwar years, when a surge in demand for recreational facilities was amplified by the prevalence of automobiles and the increasing population of the East Bay. From 1944 through 1945, Wildcat

Canyon's CCC camp had been converted into a rest center for returning soldiers who were also offered recreational activities throughout the park, including access to golfing, swimming at Lake Anza and parties at the Brazilian Room. Softball games were held at several sites in the park. In 1946, the northern end of Tilden Park was turned into a nature camp for schoolchildren (see chapter 12).

CONCESSIONS AND ACQUISITIONS

On February 25, 1947, Emery Stone reported to the board his findings from a recent trip to Los Angeles' Griffith Park, where he and Walpole had gone to observe recreational services that were provided by the city. The board subsequently approved two operations that still exist (see chapters 13, the merry-go-round, and 14, the steam train).

Other recreational activities developed in the northern end of the park during Walpole's tenure included a trout fishing pond, an archery range, tennis courts and a model airplane field. Nearby Meadows Field was being used by the public for football, soccer, softball and other sports. Between 1939 and 1965, it was the home field of the Golden Gate Cricket Club, where the team played matches against other Bay Area clubs, drawing large crowds. The result of all this recreational activity was the overcrowding of this part of the park, with traffic and parking issues galore. This was eventually solved by transferring some of these activities to other regional and city park venues. The most long-lasting concession no longer at Tilden Park was the pony ride. The popular ride was operated by five different concessionaires between 1948 and 2005. The final pony ride operators were Steve and Camy Thompson, between 1983 and 2005.

Tere and Richard Walpole in Las Vegas. *Courtesy of Mel Walpole Peters.*

During this period, the EBRPD was adding new parks to its network. The first acquisition was Anthony

Chabot Regional Park in Castro Valley in 1949, followed by Roberts Park in Oakland in 1951. In 1956, the district agreed to take over parks in Alameda County, using funding from annexations of Eden Township (Hayward) and Washington Township (Fremont) in 1958. The district manager position, now called general manager, became more and more complex.

As general manager of the park district, Walpole was provided living quarters in the residential annex attached to the Brazilian Room. Having divorced Margaret, he brought his new bride, Maria Teresa Lozano, here in 1957. Tere had been employed by the Mexican diplomatic corps prior to their marriage.

LABOR DISPUTE

At a March 1959 EBRPD Employee Association meeting, the same forum that had condemned Harold Curtiss fifteen years earlier, employees voted unanimously to seek membership in an AFL union.[181] The dispute escalated when Walpole fired two employees for their union organizing efforts, activities that he labeled "subversion."[182] For the next fourteen months, the board and general manager were immersed in the politics and legalities of recognizing the union. Employees were attempting to create pay parity between similar park positions and asking for wage increases. Other issues included the provision of a severance package for the two employees who had been fired, as well as the creation of an employee pension plan.

On June 28, 1960, Walpole surprised the board by submitting his resignation based on health reasons. He expressed his regret at leaving the position he had held for so many years.[183] The park board ultimately recognized the new union. It was one of the first such unions in a park district ever created in the state. Walpole moved his family to North Las Vegas, where he designed, built and operated a municipal nine-hole golf course. He served as the president of the Nevada Parks and Recreation Society and was supervising the completion of a scenic park when he died of a heart attack on October 7, 1973.[184]

MEMORIES AND LEGACY

Richard Eden Walpole's story has been preserved by two of his and Tere's children. His daughter Melvina (Mel) Peters retains her father's vast archives, and his other daughter, Mary S. Granen, has her father's 1937–39 diary.[185] On November 30, 2010, Pat O'Brien, then assistant general manager; park board member Doug Siden; Ciel Koplas (Walpole's secretary); Walpole family members; and park and golf course employees dedicated a plaque at Tilden golf course to honor Walpole's career.

Right: Robert Doyle, Mary Granen, Ceil Koplas and Doug Siden at 2010 event. *Below*: Memorial plaque to Richard Walpole at Tilden Park Golf Course. *Photos by the author*.

EXPLORING THE HISTORY
OF THE TILDEN NATURE AREA

Between 1935 and 1946, the 740 acres that became the Tilden Nature Area (TNA) were used by the federal government, first as a CCC campsite and then by an army camp, during the war years. In 1946, the army's lease expired, and control of the property was returned to the regional park district. Shortly after this transfer, the Oakland Unified School District secured the exclusive use of the property as an "in-town camp" and nature area.

ALAMEDA COUNTY SCHOOLS RUN TNA (1946–66)

Dave Snyder was a forty-one-year veteran of the Oakland school system as director of its physical education and recreational programs. He was the prime mover in securing the Wildcat Canyon site for use as a nature camp by Alameda County children.

Snyder had already earned a reputation for having created year-round daytime and evening sports and social programs for high school students; by the 1945–46 school years, he had increased enrollment in these programs to 487,000 students. He then founded summer "Fun Schools" for younger children to have opportunities to stay active during their school breaks.[186]

Snyder wanted to build a "Dream Camp" where children could be taught natural science while enjoying outdoor activities like hiking, swimming and camping. He worked with the EBRPD's board to form an alliance with seven school districts located in proximity to the park—Berkeley, Albany, Oakland, Piedmont, Emeryville, Alameda and San Leandro—to develop his Dream Camp.[187]

CONVERSION OF ARMY CAMP TO NATURE CAMP

By September 1946, the dream camp project was underway. Edwin Clay was hired to serve as camp manager and naturalist. He was assisted by Robert Ruel, Oakland Technical High School's shop instructor, and a small group of teenagers from Oakland High School. Among them was Ed Meese, then sixteen years old, who later became President Ronald Reagan's appointee as the seventy-fifth attorney general of the United States. Meese, a tenth grader at Oakland Junior High School, described his experience with Clay, his Boy Scout leader:

> *I actually worked up there during the summer; there were four of us employed at extremely low wages. The Army had turned it over to the park district and I remember doing a lot of things, clearing out barracks, and getting them ready for use, bringing in surplus equipment from WWII, like tables and chairs that we got from other locations. That's what the three or four of us did during the summer.*[188]

The refurbishment of the former CCC camp took six months. The repairs to the fifteen buildings included patching the foundation, rewiring, reroofing, installing new plumbing and laying down fresh paint. Jean Nelson, a general science teacher from Fremont High School, was in charge of developing a museum of natural history at the camp, and she stocked it with mounted birds and animals provided by the University of California. Public and private funding sponsored many exhibits. This new venue was named the Field Nature Museum.[189]

The nature camp opened on April 5, 1947, Easter weekend. Its objectives were to encourage children to build self-sufficiency and learn outdoor skills and to spark their interest in the natural sciences. The boys and girls renamed it "Camp Tahloma." (*Tahloma* is a native name for "wildcat.") All year round, five days a week, camp director Clay led nature classes for groups of children aged ten to seventeen. Separate sleeping quarters and camp activities were provided for boys and girls. By 1948, Clay "had acquainted approximately 2,500 children with the natural lore to be discovered in this region," reported Richard Walpole.[190]

A leadership council governed the educational policies of the camp while the park district contributed to the camp staff by hiring Tom Kennedy, an ex-Marine, to serve as special game warden. Kennedy was charged with keeping trespassers out of TNA—especially anyone bringing in firearms.[191]

There were several major changes at Camp Tahloma during 1949, its third year. First of all, it opened to the public in July for tours given by appointment from Wednesdays through Saturdays.[192]

The park hired a naturalist, Jack Parker, who conducted the public tours. According to Parker, more than sixty-eight thousand people visited TNA during its first year after opening to the public.[193] Parker served with the U.S. Forestry Department, the U.S. Fish and Wildlife Service and the California State Department of Fish and Game before joining the park district in 1948. Jack and his wife, Martha, nicknamed "Boots," lived in one of the camp's residence buildings.

Sibley, Walpole and MacDonald (*left to right*) opening the gates to the Nature Area in 1949. *Courtesy of EBRPD archives.*

In September 1949, Parker formed three new weekend nature clubs for children aged eight to twelve and invited interested youngsters to join him on his rounds of the nature area. The most prominent and long-lasting club was the Junior Rangers.[194]

Glenn Rogers was eleven when he first joined the Junior Rangers and reminisced:

> *I was in the program from 1958 to 1962. Both Jack and Boots Parker ran the program. They would lead us on hikes. Boots focused on identifying plants and birds. Jack encouraged us to learn how to play a harmonica, which I brought on the hikes. We had overnight hikes and learned to make "ranger stew" (a mixture of pot roast, gravy, water, and potatoes) that was delicious. He had that a slow southern drawl; I think he was from Mississippi. He played things a little "loosey-goosey," letting us run all around the trails, but kept us involved.*[195]

In 1999, participants in the Junior Rangers celebrated a fiftieth reunion of the club's founding with a theme of "50 Years of Mud, Sweat and Cheers." Alumni of Parker's program renewed old friendships and relived their experiences, which they claimed had given them a lifelong love of nature.[196]

In October, the Alameda County school system changed naturalists: Sylvan Wall replaced Clay as director of the nature camp. Wall had majored in forestry at UC Berkeley and served as a California park ranger for seven years, blazing trails from the southern end of the state to its northern border. He and his wife, Peggy, raised their two daughters in one of the TNA residences.[197]

Josh Barkin, naturalist, interpretive specialist. *Courtesy of EBRPD archives.*

Throughout the early 1950s, the two programs—one facilitated by Wall and the other by Parker—continued to bring children into the park for nature study. Josh Barkin was hired in 1960 and advanced from assistant naturalist to naturalist to interpretive specialist over a twenty-year career. He was recognized nationally for his interpretive skills. "He was a delightful man who really liked working with kids," said Nancy McKay of the park district.

Right: Jack Parker, first TNA naturalist. *Courtesy of EBRPD archives*.

Below: Sylvan Wall, director of Nature Camp. *Courtesy of EBRPD archives*.

LITTLE FARM

Tilden Park's famous Little Farm opened on June 7, 1955. Its working barn was constructed by sixteen boys from Berkeley High School's Vocational Carpentry Class under the supervision of their teacher, Walter H. Miller, trade and industrial coordinator of Berkeley Schools. It was designed by Berkeley Kiwanis Club member Albert Hunter Jr., who provided $1,500 to purchase the building materials. The barn is on a five-eighths scale to what would be a typical structure in "real life." At the dedication, the Little Farm animal residents were introduced; these included burros, sheep, a pig, goats, rabbits, pigeons, chickens and a peacock.

Park ranger Maryanne Danielson, Tilden Little Farm. *Courtesy of EBRPD archives.*

JEWEL LAKE

Jewel Lake is located along the Jewel Lake Trail about a quarter mile north of the Little Farm. It was created much earlier than any other part of the Tilden Nature Area. In 1921, the East Bay Water Company, intending to create a reservoir, diverted Wildcat Creek water through the San Pablo tunnel and

Jewel Lake, 1940. *Courtesy of EBRPD archives.*

built a small dam. Due to the lake's abundance of clay particles, the water turned out to be unusable as a source of drinking water. Nevertheless, the one-acre pond became a splendid habitat for plant and animal life, attracting migrating water birds and providing a year-round home for numerous turtles. Birders find the nature trail to and from Jewel Lake, which winds through oak forest, to be a great spot for sighting songbirds.

NATURE LODGE

The long-awaited Junior Ranger Nature Lodge finally opened in July 1956 after a two-year do-it-yourself effort by staff, assisted by Junior Rangers themselves. Members of the park board joined over three hundred celebrants at the opening ceremony. The lodge, located just north of the Little Farm, had museum exhibits on everything from honeybees to the geology of the Jewel Lake and displays of wildflowers, butterflies and insects.[198]

SCHOOL PROGRAM TERMINATED

The dual efforts of naturalists Parker and Wall continued until 1966, when the school program was the victim of budget cuts.[199] During the program's previous twenty years, over 100,000 public school pupils had been able to see and touch plants during four thousand field trips. The success of the programs had continued despite of the loss of Martha "Boots" Parker, who passed away around 1963. Martha had contributed to the programming along with her husband, and she was memorialized in the new Nature Center erected in 1974.[200]

***

A summary of the contributions of key members of Tilden Park's nature program leadership over the last fifty-three years:

CHRIS NELSON, CHIEF OF INTERPRETATION, CHIEF OF PARKS AND INTERPRETATION (1962–89)

Nelson completed his bachelor's degree at Michigan State in zoology and a master's at Oregon State University in wildlife management and conservation. He had been working at the Sacramento Junior Museum, a

Chris Nelson, chief of interpretation. *Courtesy of EBRPD archives.*

children's nature center, as a fill-in job, when in walked Bill Mott, the new general manager of the park district. Mott asked a lot of questions, then invited Chris to come to Oakland to discuss setting up a new interpretive department for the district. He was chief of interpretation, then chief of parks and interpretation, for the last twenty years of his career.[201]

When Chris began working for the district, the East Bay school program was foundering as a result of budget cutbacks. This allowed Chris to negotiate for the park district to run the program, add staff and eventually to house the program in the new interpretive center, rather than the old drafty CCC buildings. The first thing that was done was to survey the schools' curriculum needs for each grade to see how the out-of-doors served their needs. Chris hired additional staff (including Tim Gordon, Ron Russo and Alan Kaplan) and worked with them to develop all kinds of teaching aides to spark the program, using more hands-on activities in which the kids could participate and less lecturing from the naturalists.

Building the Environmental Education Center

It took five years to get board approval for the project and another three to get the Environmental Education Center (EEC) completed and ready for its dedication. Chris said he used his experience visiting hundreds of nature centers, his own ideas and those of staff to come up with an innovative and architecturally sound design. At that point, there was resistance from environmental groups, including the Sierra Club, to cutting down the

Eleven-thousand-square-foot Environmental Education Center. *Photo by John Hartz, Exhibit Lab; courtesy of EBRPD archives.*

eucalyptus trees to clear space for the center, and spending money on buildings rather than buying more land for additional parks. A budget of $600,000 and an environmental justification report were created, as well as a name change, from an interpretive center to the Environmental Education Center, to facilitate passage through the legislature. A funding campaign was led by Clyde Woolridge; Chevron USA, Mervyn's and the Oakland Lions Club stepped forward with contributions. The dedication was held on October 24, 1974, coinciding with the fortieth anniversary of the East Bay Regional Park District.[202]

RON RUSSO, NATURALIST (1966–69), SUPERVISING NATURALIST (1969–79), CHIEF OF INTERPRETATION AND AQUATICS (1997–2004)

After earning a bachelor's degree from Sacramento State University in park management in 1965, Ron went to work for the City of Palo Alto as a ranger-naturalist there for around a year before transferring to the East Bay Regional Park District.

At the time, there were only two rangers (naturalists) at the Nature Area.... Josh Barkin and Jack Parker. They wore the old heavy woolen uniforms with red bandanas around their necks. I thought the whole operation, especially the Little Farm, was pretty hokey. Little did I know I would start working there in 1966, fall in love with the place, and shortly become area supervisor. I was in Tilden for 14 years, from 1966–1980.

Once I started working there and seeing how important the Little Farm was to urban kids who never saw cows and pigs, I thought it was the greatest thing next to sliced bread, so to speak. In the beginning, the farm was for display only. Once I took it over, I turned it into a breeding facility with calves and lambs born annually. It was just magical timing. I remember for three years in a row, we had a calf born on a Sunday afternoon when the farm was packed with families.... One event in particular drew about 400 people. Folks were calling their neighbors and telling them to get down there quick.

When I first started there the rule was that we did programs for children only during the week. No one did any weekend programs for the general public. Tim and I decided to ignore the rule and start offering programs for the public and we routinely asked folks to let the park board know if they

Ron Russo, TNA supervising naturalist. *Courtesy of EBRPD archives.*

liked the experimental service. *The board was flooded with complimentary letters, so we couldn't get into trouble for ignoring the rule. And that's how seven day a week service started in the district.*

This was the era when we basically established most of the interpretive department's core values, teaching strategies and preparation requirements… in effect the standards of operation which would become critical to the entire staff for the next 40 years. It helped spawn many ground-breaking programs and it earned the district's naturalists a national reputation for excellence.[203]

STEVE ABBORS,
TNA SUPERVISING NATURALIST (1979–84)

After earning a master's in biological sciences from California State University–East Bay, Steve began his professional career with the East Bay Regional Park District in February 1971 at the Lake Chabot boat rental concession stand. He worked at Chabot and Coyote Hills as a naturalist aide before transferring to Tilden Nature Area in the summer of 1974.

We spent most of the summer of 1974 preparing the newly completed Environmental Education Center for the grand opening on October 24th. I gave the first public program at the EEC entitled "Great Whales and other Pet Foods." The consciousness about whaling had really blossomed and this was a subject that really engaged the public. The EEC was a fascinating place to work during the decade I worked there. We did a lot a public education around fairly new subjects such as integrated pest management and permaculture. Tim Gordon, who started at TNA before nearly all of us, championed many of these new ideas.

In September 1979, I was promoted to supervising naturalist. Chris Nelson, our department head, promoted me both times. The naturalists I worked with were Josh Barkin, Ron Russo, Tim Gordon, Linda Yemoto, Alan Kaplan, Simone Dangles, and Peter Ourusoff.

My wife Carlene and I moved into the park residence adjacent to the EEC in 1980, after Josh Barkin left due to failing health. Our second daughter Rose was born when we were living there and life at the EEC had a huge impact on both Rose and her older sister Alison. Before either of

Steve Abbors, TNA
supervising naturalist.
*Midpeninsula Regional Open
Space, www.openspace.org*

them turned 4 years old, they were familiar with all of the farm animals at the Little Farm, which they visited daily. I was always delighted to see Carlene wander through the office on the way to the EEC rotunda carrying Rose and holding Alison by the hand. Ali referred to everyone who worked at the EEC as the "Center People." Because she had no neighbors, Ali became skilled at striking up conversations with young children who came to the EEC with their parents, and often invited them over to the residence to have them act out parts in small plays she dreamed up.

In 1984 I joined the East Bay Municipal Utility District and managed 28,000 acres of watershed land for water quality protection and recreation. Since 2008 I've served as general manager for the Midpeninsula Regional Open Space District.[204]

Steve retired from Midpen at the end of 2017. Recently, the park board announced that the former Rancho Antonio Open Space Preserve Trail was renamed the Stephen E. Abbors Trail, reported as a well-deserved honor.

MARGARET KELLEY,
TNA SUPERVISING NATURALIST (1984–2005)

"Kelley" (as she is known to her friends and "MK" to staff) has loved being in nature from her early childhood. Her dad was a forestry major at Cal. He took every opportunity to get escape to unspoiled nature. Kelley spent hours as a child with her family in the East Bay Parks, including spending the night! She was a "drop in" with Junior Rangers.

Margaret Kelley, TNA supervising naturalist. *Courtesy of EBRPD archives.*

I earned my BA in Environmental Studies & Public Relations/Journalism from San Jose State University in 1972. Between 1973 and 1980 I served as a ranger-naturalist at Sequoia National Park, CA and had several research & supervisory assignments for public and private agencies in San Jose, CA and Portland, Oregon while concurrently earning my MA Natural Sciences and teaching credential from San Jose State University.

I started my EBRPD career as a naturalist at Coyote Hills (1980-84) and was promoted to supervising naturalist at the Tilden Nature Area, serving from 1984-2005. During that time (1995-2005) I served on the park district steering committee responsible for founding Camp Arroyo (2001), and was its outdoor education manager for that year.

I then served as interpretive services manager for the park district between 2005 and 2007. I now live in Sedona, Arizona.[205]

DAVE ZUCKERMANN,
TNA SUPERVISING NATURALIST (2005–14)

I have a BA in Sociology from UC Berkeley. I got my start with the district in the early 80s as a docent/volunteer at Sunol Regional Wilderness, then went on to work as an Interpretive Student Aide at Tilden Nature Area from 1983 to 1984. I gained valuable naturalist experience working for the LA schools' outdoor education center in the San Gabriel Mountains and for Sacramento County Parks and Recreation before returning to the district in 1987. I served as a naturalist at Ardenwood for a few years and then at Tilden Nature Area for almost 16 years. In 2005, I was promoted to supervising naturalist at the Tilden Nature Area, overseeing the Little Farm, park operations and interpretive programming, including the historic Tilden Junior Ranger program.[206]

Dave Zuckermann, TNA supervising naturalist. *Photo by the author.*

In 2015, Dave was promoted to manager of interpretative and recreational services for the northwest region after serving a year as acting manager.

SARA FETTERLY,
CURRENT TNA SUPERVISING NATURALIST

I began working for the park district in the spring of 2001 at Ardenwood Historic Farm. After 10 years of potato planting and tomato tasting, I traded in my pitchfork for binoculars and moved to Crab Cove where I spent five beautiful years at the edge of the bay.

Sara Fetterly, Current TNA
Supervising Naturalist.
Photo by the author.

But once a farm girl, always a farm girl, and in 2015 I happily accepted a position as supervising naturalist of the Tilden Nature Area and Little Farm. Prior to EBRPD, I held a variety of job titles including wildlife biologist, environmental consultant, and Peace Corps volunteer. I have a BA degree in Environmental Geography from San Diego State University and a Master of Education from University of San Francisco. In my spare time I love traveling, hiking, camping, snowboarding, and spending time with my family.[207]

CURRENT NATURE SIGHTINGS

In the entryway of the Environmental Education Building is a whiteboard where the public is invited to record the names of wildlife that they have encountered on their walks around the Nature Area. Common sightings include red-tailed hawks, turkey vultures, loons, bufflehead ducks, snowy egrets, western and slider turtles and an occasional fox or coyote. Rarer still were recent sightings of a red crossbill and a river otter.

JUNIOR RANGER PROGRAM

The Junior Ranger program is conducted during the school year for selected kids. Other seasonal day camps for children include:

TILDEN TOTS for ages three to four, each accompanied by an adult

TILDEN EXPLORERS for ages five to seven, each may be accompanied by an adult

TILDEN MINI-RANGERS for ages eight to thirteen, unaccompanied by parents

A full list of adult and children's programs can be found at www.ebrps.org/parks/tilden/tna.

2017 TNA USAGE STATISTICS OF VISITORS ATTENDING TNA PROGRAMS[208]

- Naturalists did 273 school programs at Tilden. A total of 7,601 kids were served.
- 347 "Regional in Nature" (RIN) programs were attended by 12,837 people.
- 7,675 people enjoyed private or impromptu programs with Tilden Interpretive staff at the park (non-RIN, non-school groups).
- 9 programs were held outside the regional parks in schools, libraries and community centers, serving a total of 357 people.
- 3 open house events were held in 2017 attended by 4,077 people.
- In 2017, Tilden Nature Area had 35 docents who provided 1,314 hours of volunteer service.

Sara Fetterly acknowledged that the usage statistics exclude "unmonitored casual visitors," for example, those on self-guided tours of the Environmental Education Center and Little Farm, those hiking around Jewel Lake's boardwalk and those on extended hikes or bicycle rides along the TNA's ten miles of trails, who add significantly to the visitor count, making the Tilden Nature Area one of the most highly utilized areas within the greater Tilden Regional Park.

STORY OF THE TILDEN
MERRY-GO-ROUND

THE PARK DISTRICT'S FIRST AMUSEMENT RIDE

In 1947, the park board instigated action to bring recreational concessions to Tilden Park. District manager Walpole contacted Ross Davis, the carousel operator for Griffith Park in Los Angeles, to arrange a meeting. In February, Walpole and EBRPD director Emery Stone traveled south to Griffith Park, a park with similar topography to Tilden. Walpole and Davis were not strangers; Walpole was superintendent of Griffith Park's golf courses adjacent to the carousel facility before coming to Tilden. He knew that Davis had an extra carousel in storage and wanted to explore the possibility of Davis bringing it to operate in Tilden Park.

Davis's 1911 Herschell–Spillman menagerie merry-go-round was installed in Griffith Park in the summer of 1935 while a permanent carousel building was under construction. When the new building was completed, the carousel moved inside, but not for long. The ride proved to be so popular that the 1911 three-row carousel was replaced by a four-row 1926 Spillman and the three-row machine went into storage.

Davis responded favorably to Walpole's idea. After a brief visit to Berkeley, Davis indicated that the best location for the merry-go-round would be on a hillside midway between the Meadows picnic area and Lake Anza. In May 1947, Walpole and Stone were authorized by the park district to make arrangements with Davis for the installation.

Walpole designed the layout for the carousel, and his secretary Carolyn Thatcher executed this drawing. *Courtesy of EBRPD archives.*

Completed carousel, 1950. *Courtesy of EBRPD archives.*

The four-year contract negotiated with Davis required the park to prepare the site, which involved the construction of the merry-go-round building as well as a food concession. This entailed removing a grove of eucalyptus trees, cutting off the top of the hill and extensive grading. A new half-mile road, Central Park Drive, also had to be constructed. Finally, it required the paving of a parking lot and construction of a restroom.

On Saturday, May 29, 1948, the new merry-go-round opened to great fanfare. During its first month of operation, the merry-go-round had forty thousand riders. Receipts from food concession sales totaled $3,000. It was a rousing start!

THE DAVIS FAMILY: THREE GENERATIONS OF MERRY-GO-ROUND MEN

Ross Davis represented the second of three generations of legendary merry-go-round operators. In 1900, his father, Oliver F. Davis, came with his family to Redlands, California, to work as a builder. After receiving a small portable carousel as payment for a debt, he decided to take the carousel on the road with traveling carnivals. Oliver and his brother Howard became "Davis Bros. Auto Merry Go Round." They traveled by rail and wagon. When Howard grew tired of the life, Oliver's son Ross stepped in to replace him. After ten years on the road, the Davis family was ready to secure a permanent installation for their merry-go-round business. In 1910, they installed a three-row Herschell-Spillman merry-go-round in Luna Park in Los Angeles and, in 1913, relocated it to San Diego. That carousel still operates just outside of the San Diego Zoo.

The Tilden merry-go-round was the second permanent unit that the Davises ordered from the Herschell-Spillman Company in North Tonawanda, New York, near Niagara Falls. Purchased in 1911, the new merry-go-round served briefly in three Southern California locations before it arrived at Tilden.

Allan Herschell had been one of the top names in the industry since completing his first carousel in 1883. The partnership with his brother-in-law Edward Spillman was formed in 1903. Nearly half of all classic wooden carousels manufactured in the United States and still in operation were manufactured by one of the Herschell-Spillman companies.[209]

Body makers at work, Herschell-Spellman Company, North Tonawanda, New York. *Courtesy of Herschell Factory Museum.*

While Ross Davis managed the family's Southern California merry-go-round concessions, his son John O. Davis and John's wife, Janet, were the first operators of the carousel at Tilden Park. Beginning in 1948, they lived in an apartment next to the carousel and started their family. John and Janet shut down the carousel for almost a year in 1950 to enlarge it by adding a fourth inner row of animals made of cast aluminum. The platform was extended into the center of the machine to support the additional row and a new cornice was added, painted by Nate Bolias, an old carny sign painter

Jeanette and Harry Perry.
Courtesy of EBRPD archives.

whom Davis employed. Bolias continued to paint and retouch the animals until his death at age ninety-three.

In 1953, the Davises moved back to Los Angeles to run their family's businesses there. Jan's favorite cousin, Harry O. Perry, and his wife, Jeanette, took over the Tilden operation. The Perrys became a one-third owner of the Tilden merry-go-round and were sole operators for the next thirty-nine years.

Prior to World War II, Harry worked in an oil field; during the war, he was an airplane mechanic. After the war, Harry, his father and brother-in-law Paul Steele owned a hardware store in Saticoy, Ventura County. "All this mechanical knowledge and bookkeeping experience of the hardware business worked into what I did at the merry-go-round." While Harry took care of most aspects of the merry-go-round business, Jeanette's main role was raising their three children.

1976 PARK ACQUISITION OF THE MERRY-GO-ROUND

A decline in ticket sales for the merry-go-round led to changes in the management of one of Tilden Park's star attractions. As former park district assistant general manager Jerry Kent explained it:

*Our annual rides were about 200,000 per year until the seventies. It got
down to 140,000 in 1975 due to parking and circulation issues within
the park (mainly because of the swimmers at nearby Lake Anza taking
up merry-go-round parking spots)....Lake Anza and Lake Temescal were
the only two lake swimming areas in all of the East Bay for 1.5 million
people. Parking at the merry-go-round during the summer was difficult, but
the District soon solved that problem; there are now nine swimming areas
spread out over the two counties and no parking issues up at Tilden.*

Due to the financial strain that the reduction in ticket sales had on
the business, a protracted negotiation between the park board and the
Perrys ensued in 1976. The park district expressed satisfaction with the
way Harry Perry had operated the facility. The district quickly approved
a requested fee increase and then considered Perry's offer to sell the
ride outright if they could get a contract to operate the ride. During
the controversy over the ride's selling price, the community pressure
influenced the State Historical Commission to include the Tilden merry-
go-round in the National Register of Historic Places, to ensure that
the ride wouldn't be dismantled and sold in parts (a threat that Harry
Perry had made). After a lengthy period of negotiation, a Contra Costa
Superior Court judge was called in to mediate. He ruled that the two
sides split the difference between competing valuations and ordered the
sale to be completed immediately.[210]

In 1978, the park obtained a $40,000 federal grant along with private
donations for restoration needed after thirty years in operation. This work
was carried out by Tobin Fraley's Redbug Workshop in Berkeley.

FROM PERRYS TO TERRI

The Perrys continued to operate the merry-go-round for another twenty
years under two sequential ten-year agreements with the park district. At the
end of 1992, Harry Perry announced his retirement.

Into that void stepped Terri Oyarzun, a former probation officer with
Contra Costa County, ready to give up her old job after sixteen years and
wade into the unknown. Oyarzun described how making the shift from
serving as a "cop" probation officer to running the concession affected her:

It took me around 90 days to realize that I wasn't responsible for everyone's behavior—if they drove in the exit to the parking lot or did anything wrong, I could always call the park police, and say "Help, I'm the merry-go-round operator." I didn't have to be a disciplinarian for anybody. I just had to present this wonderful environment for families who want to make memories.[211]

The Perrys helped with the transition before they finally retired and moved to Vallejo.

RENOVATIONS

By the 1990s, the merry-go-round was attracting 150,000 riders per year. It was time to call the "carousel doctor," Dan Horenberger, owner of Brass Ring Entertainment, a carousel restoration company. Starting in 2002 and for the next six years, the machinery and structure went through a top-to-bottom overhaul. The ride was closed for three months at the beginning of 2002 while the cranks and bearings were replaced with more highly engineered parts in compliance with government safety requirements. The gift shop/food concession and the apartment structure for the merry-go-round operators were also upgraded over this three-month period.

The East Bay Regional Park District Foundation completed the second phase of the restoration process in 2007, which included a new state-of-the-art weatherproof glass enclosure, a new platform and a complete restoration of the antique North Tonawanda Band Organ. The Tilden merry-go-round is actually equipped with two band organs. The smaller one is the North Tonawanda Band Organ, which is mounted in the center of the carousel and was originally used during the week; the second one, a much larger band organ, was used only on holidays and Sundays.

During the Perry era, Harry accommodated the complaints of people who lived uphill from Tilden Park by muffling the organ pipes with a blanket. In 2007, the newly installed weatherproof glass shield enclosed and protected the carousel machinery from foggy and rainy weather, but the glass had an unexpected consequence. The sound levels of the band organs exceeded code levels, and the organs had to shut down. All the rolls of vintage sheet music went into storage and were replaced with recorded carousel music.

OYARZUN YEARS

Terri Oyarzun frequently expressed her joy at having spent twenty-two years as the carousel operator from 1993 until 2014. She raised her son Zephyr in the merry-go-round's apartment until he was ten years old. They interacted with a small community of families that lived in or near the park. Her husband, Egon, managed their second business, called "Goats-R-Us," which provides brush-clearing services for public and private property owners.[212]

Oyarzun counted herself fortunate to have had a second family of dedicated employees; some were inherited from the Perrys, but others started as teenagers looking for summer employment who returned year after year. A few made the merry-go-round a big part of their career.

Oyarzun became aware of special needs children and adults who took delight in the sounds and rhythms of the ride. Along with a third group of family and friends, she hosted a month-long Christmas Fantasy celebration that started the Friday after Thanksgiving and lasted until Christmas Eve. A core group of friends came together to help with the decorations, making them more and more elaborate every year for fifteen straight years.

Terri Oyarzun with her husband, Egon, in front of carousel. *Courtesy of Terri Oyarzun.*

CENTENNIAL CELEBRATION

To celebrate the 100th anniversary of the merry-go-round, Oyarzun asked me to produce a book describing the rich history of the ride. *Tilden Regional Park Merry-Go-Round: 100 Years of Spinning Dreams* was well received.[213] On July 13, 2011, a large crowd of frolicking children and their parents attended a ceremony moderated by members of the park board.

THE KWASNICKI FAMILY, THE NEW CONCESSIONAIRES

In 2013, Terri Oyarzun's second ten-year concession contract expired, and the EBRPD decided to put the new contract out to bid. After reviewing competitive proposals, the concession was awarded to a new contractor. Oyarzun, initially saddened by the loss of the contract, eventually came to terms with the change in her life after the more than two decades she had devoted to the merry-go-round operation. "It was time," she said. She and her family continue to run Goats-R-Us out of their two-hundred-acre ranch in Martinez.

Steven and Doreen Kwasnicki began their contract as the new merry-go-round concession operator in May 2014. Both had grown up riding

Doreen, Megan and Steve Kwasnicki. *Photo by the author.*

Tilden's carousel; Steve had lived in Berkeley, less than two miles away, and Doreen in Albany, about three miles away. They are delighted to have returned to the scene of their favorite childhood recreation site.

Steve's career journey started twenty-five years ago, operating a landscaping company. He and a couple of close friends formed a company, Sycamore Concessions, to bid on landscape contracts for new markets in the East Bay suburbs. Doreen's career was oriented toward food service. A graduate of Le Cordon Bleu Culinary Academy, she operated first a saloon, then a restaurant, in Columbia, a charming gold rush town in the heart of the Mother Lode, about 140 miles away. After a few years in the mountains, they couldn't wait to get back to Berkeley.

Doreen and Steve's daughter Megan is a graduate of Le Cordon Bleu Culinary Academy as well. With a young assistant, Albert Rivera, Megan has formed a two-generation team to operate the merry-go-round. The operation not only requires getting children on and off the ride safely, it also involves a disciplined program of maintenance, accounting and food concession management. The team has a healthy relationship with the park district they expect to maintain for many years to come.

14

ALL ABOARD THE
TILDEN STEAM TRAINS

W hen turning into the steam train complex in the southern portion of the park, one approaches two different miniature train operations. The first is the Redwood Valley Railway, and below it is the Golden Gate Live Steamers Club. This chapter tells the history of both.

REDWOOD VALLEY RAILWAY

When it was created in 1952, the name of this facility was the Tilden South Gate and Pacific Railway. The name was changed to the Redwood Valley Railway in July 1971 when an extension of the railroad was built, tripling the size of its route through the park. Since the first whistle blew on May 8, 1952, either Erich Thomsen or his daughter Ellen Thomsen has been at the helm, building and operating the steam train that has brought joy to millions of riders. Both young and old have flocked to this historic narrow-gauge railroad over the last sixty-seven years.[214]

Erich Thomsen was born in Hamburg, Germany, in 1920. His father was a brick- and stonemason. In 1927, the Thomsen family, including Erich and his three brothers, immigrated to the United States and settled in San Francisco. Erich graduated from Lick Wilmerding High School in 1937, fully trained in mechanical drawing and civil engineering. He enrolled at San Francisco State University but left before graduation to take a job with Southern Pacific Railroad as a fireman on steam engines. He later worked for Yuba Manufacturing Company, designing gold-dredging equipment. He married his wife, Adell, in 1947 and in 1948 went to work for the Western Pacific Railroad as a mechanical engineer and track inspector.

In the mid-1940s, Thomsen began a miniature train hobby by laying out a short track in the backyard of his parents' farm in Mountain View. Over the course of the next few years, he joined other vintage narrow-gauge enthusiasts in the Railway and Locomotive Historical Society. Some were turning their hobby into businesses. Thomsen nurtured this ambition but did not have the funds to develop a workable site.

Erich Thomsen, Redwood Valley Railway owner. *Thomsen family archives.*

Thomsen learned that Richard Walpole was interested in adding a miniature passenger train line to Tilden Park's attractions and submitted a design for a one-third-scale model of an old-time narrow-gauge railroad that featured an 1875 American Standard locomotive engine. It was to be located at the south end of the park and would produce returns comparable to similar steam train operations elsewhere. The park board immediately approved this proposal and authorized Walpole to draw up a contract that would take effect on September 1, 1951. Park workers completed the grading required for a parking area, station building and track layout at the site by the South Gate entrance to the park.

TILDEN, SOUTH GATE AND PACIFIC RAILWAY CREATED

Thomsen formed a brief partnership with Jack Campbell, manager of the Acme Welding Company. Thomsen and Campbell did all the welding and blacksmithing jobs in their spare time. The railway was a twelve-inch-gauge layout, half a mile long. Nine tons of steel rails, three thousand redwood ties and one hundred tons of crushed rock ballast were used to finish the roadbed. Upon completion of the railway in 1952, Thomsen bought out Campbell's interest in the business.

Directors Roberts at the throttle, MacDonald and Sibley behind him at opening of the Tilden Steam Train in 1952. *Courtesy of EBRPD archives.*

On June 15, 1952, the ride was given a preview when the public was invited to ride the new train for free. Over eight hundred passengers, both children and adults, took advantage of the opportunity. An invitation-only preview was held for the park district board on August 16 to mark the official opening. In addition to the rides, free ice cream and soft drinks were offered to more than one thousand guests and their families.

The Tilden, South Gate and Pacific Railway was enormously popular from its beginning. For its first fifteen years of operation, it remained unchanged. Thomsen kept his weekday engineering and inspector's job with the Western Pacific Railroad Company, working in the company's San Francisco office, but he moved his family to Berkeley to be closer to his miniature railroad business. In the basement of his Magnolia Street home, Thomsen completed a new engine in 1965. Engine No. 4, "Laurel," a five-inch-scale, fifteen-inch-gauge 2-4-2 was his original design and had been on the drawing boards since 1954.

THE ARMY CAMP EXTENSION

The next major change in the steam train operation came in November 1959 when the army officially abandoned its South Park Army Camp lease. Many alternative uses of the abandoned army camp area were proposed, including a picnic site, playfields and a swimming pool.

On July 1, 1962, William Penn Mott assumed the general manager position. He would have a major impact on Tilden Park as well as the entire park district. After meeting with Thomsen and representatives of the Golden Gate Live Steamers Club who were operating exhibition trains in Redwood Park, Mott introduced the concept of using the abandoned army camp at the south end of Tilden to concentrate the two railroad facilities into one area. In December 1962, the board approved the train complex proposal for the two operations and authorized the preparation of a cost analysis and engineering master plan. The Golden Gate Live Steamers Club would not execute its portion of the plan for more than a decade.

Thomsen prepared his own master plan for his portion of the site's development and started building a larger engine. He also purchased materials, anticipating that the park's share of the project would be authorized, which it was, on October 8, 1968. The grading for the expanded area and installation of a tunnel under South Park Drive was completed cooperatively by Thomsen and the park district. Construction of the track extension for the new railroad was finally completed in July 1971 with volunteer labor managed by Thomsen.

RAILWAY'S NEXT GENERATION

In 1995, Erich Thomsen passed away and his daughter Ellen took the helm of this sixty-year-old family business. Thomsen's legacy is best exemplified by the locomotives, buildings, tracks and landscaping that he built for the public's enjoyment. The Redwood Valley Railway is a working museum that models and exhibits the railways of the past and serves well beyond its capacity as an attraction for Tilden Park.

Ray Pimlott, now in his eighties, has contributed to the operation for more than thirty-five years. While he worked as an electrical technician for Chevron Corporation for thirty-four years until his 1992 retirement, he moonlighted on the weekends for fifteen years at Redwood Valley Railway.

Left: Ellen Thomsen, current RVR owner. *Thomsen family archives.*

Right: Ray Pimlott, engineer for more than thirty-five years. *Photo by the author.*

Ray Pimlott working on Engine No. 5. *Courtesy of E.E. Thomsen.*

One of his tasks, which took fourteen years, was building locomotive no. 7, finally put into service in 2006.[215] As he explained it, the Redwood Valley is "a hobby that got out of hand."[216]

REDWOOD VALLEY RAILWAY TODAY

Thomsen and his successors built four engines: the No. 4 Laurel, the No. 5 Fern, the No. 7 Oak and the No. 11 Sequoia. When public demand grew, they also built a fleet of cars. In 2015, the privately owned Redwood Valley Railway set a new passenger record, carrying 205,000 customers. It continues to be one of the leading recreational attractions in the entire East Bay Regional Park District.

The loyal crew of employees and trainees operate like a family—and, in fact, several of these trainees are sons or daughters of current or former crew members, carrying forward the spirit instilled by founder Erich Thomsen.

Redwood Valley Railway Engine No. 7 controlled by Jerry Nicholson. *Photo by the author.*

GOLDEN GATE LIVE STEAMERS (GGLS)

The second miniature operation in the complex is the Golden Gate Live Steamers Club. It is the oldest of more than sixty live steam railway clubs in the country.[217] Victor Shattock organized the club in 1936 in his basement in Oakland's Fruitvale neighborhood. Shattock had purchased the house in 1934 and dug a thirty-two-by-forty-five-foot basement, large enough to install a large model of a working railroad. The track ran all the way around the basement walls and included an electrically operated turntable, a water tank and a string of freight cars.

VICTOR SHATTOCK

Shattock was born in Devonshire, England, in 1886, one of eight children whose father was a stationmaster for the Great Western Railway. In his teens, Victor immigrated to Calgary, Canada. He served in the Canadian army in World War I and was stationed in France, where he was assigned the task of repairing railroads damaged during the fighting. He moved to California in 1923 and started working for the Southern Pacific Railroad in Niles. He

Victor Shattock, club organizer. *Courtesy of EBRPD archives.*

moved several times in the 1930s before finding the ideal home in Oakland where he could install his live steam railroad. By the late 1940s, he was the water service foreman for the Southern Pacific.[218]

A club was formed by the dozen members who met monthly at Victor's home to operate his half-inch-scale live steam trains as well as the miniatures by other club members. The original name of the club was the East Bay Engineer's Society. As membership and the scale of equipment grew, the club eventually moved to outdoor facilities, although the basement track continued in service for twenty-seven years.

REDWOOD REGIONAL PARK SITE

A February 1948 letter from Frank Dee of the Golden Gate Live Steamers Club to the EBRPD board suggested that the board consider permitting the model rail group to operate its miniature trains in Redwood Regional Park, thereby creating a public attraction and aiding efforts to attract a new younger group to the hobby. The board unanimously agreed to grant the Live Steamer's Club an opportunity to demonstrate its unusual avocation to the public and to maintain a workshop in Redwood Regional Park.[219]

Club members started laying the 1,330 feet of track needed for the project on weekends. The club was assisted by the park district, which had graded the plot of land, and by the Southern Pacific Railroad, which had furnished lumber for ties and engineers to draw up professional plans. The track accommodated three sizes of locomotives: $2\frac{1}{2}$-, $3\frac{1}{2}$- and $4\frac{3}{4}$-inch gauge.[220] The track had a 6-by-6-foot-long transfer table that was used to move the engines to the operating track.

The twenty-five club members included professional railroaders and tradesmen. All were hobbyists who built replicas of standard-gauge steam-powered locomotives. In 1949, this group bestowed honorary membership on Richard Walpole, Wesley Adams and John MacDonald from the EBRPD, as well as on eight members of the Southern Pacific. The 1953 roster boasted trainmen from Berkeley, San Leandro, Orinda, Lafayette, Oakland, San Francisco, Walnut Creek, Alameda and even peninsula cities.

The track officially opened with a Golden Spike Ceremony on September 2, 1950. The August 1957 issue of the club newsletter called the *Callboy* noted that the club had the longest $2\frac{1}{2}$-inch-gauge track in the world.

Golden Spike Ceremony in Redwood Park, 1950. *Courtesy of EBRPD archives.*

What size the track should be was an issue that had caused internal conflict in the club for years. It was finally determined that the 7½ gauge, which had taken hold as the standard hobby gauge on the West Coast, would be adopted by the club at Redwood. In May 1961, construction was underway on the new larger gauge track at Redwood Park.

By the end of 1962, the question had arisen as to the possibility of moving the entire operation to Tilden Park. William Penn Mott had given a presentation at the club's December meeting in which he discussed the pros and cons of such a move. The two principal problems of remaining at Redwood Park were the very limited usable level area for track expansion and the road congestion caused by the popularity of the facility.

MOVE TO TILDEN PARK

By the March 1963 board meeting, the Golden Gate Club had informed the board that it unanimously approved the proposal to move to Tilden. Years went by. The club continued to occupy the Redwood Park site while it debated all aspects of a move to Tilden, including the height, length and gauge of the new track. Finally, in 1971, the club began moving its track system into the Tilden Park site, where the park district had graded and installed drainage.

Construction work continued for several more years. It was not until September 1975 that the Golden Spike Ceremony was performed before an audience of several hundred people, with an attending complement of more than forty locomotives. The ceremony also dedicated the completion of the Heintz Loop, named after Ralph Heintz, a club member who had donated some four thousand feet of rail and other materials to the Tilden project.

Ralph Heinz, 1975 Golden Spike Ceremony in Tilden Park. *Courtesy of EBRPD archives.*

GGLS TODAY

GGLS is a nonprofit corporation, a 501(c)(3) museum, whose mission is to operate a large-scale miniature railroad and promote craftsmanship in model engineering for the benefit of members and the education of the public. The GGLS track accommodates four gauges: $2\frac{1}{2}$, $3\frac{1}{2}$, $4\frac{3}{4}$ and $7\frac{1}{2}$ inches.[221] The scales are $\frac{1}{2}$, $\frac{3}{4}$, 1 and $1\frac{1}{2}$ inches to the foot.

All the work and maintenance on the equipment and facility is done by club members, who work as volunteers. Members with home shop

Top: Families on GGLS ride. *Left*: GGLS club members observing work on Engine 22. *Photos by the author.*

machining facilities construct their own equipment. Other builders purchase castings and other supplies from vendors serving the hobby.

The following Yelp review sums it up:

> *The Golden Gate Live Steamers is a miniature train hobby club. Open Sundays giving rides from 12:00-3:00 pm, they strive to expand the growth of the live steam hobby for generations to come. Running on a donation basis, a quick 6 minute ride behind a 7.5" gauge real working steam locomotive gives a great tour of the facilities and of a wonderful view of the greenery in Tilden Park. It's a great opportunity to learn about steam trains and also a great way to spend your Sunday with your family.*

PART IV

PREPARING THE PARK
FOR THE FUTURE

REMEMBERING
WILLIAM PENN MOTT JR.

Sometime after Richard Walpole's resignation in June 1960, Dr. Robert Gordon Sproul, former president of the University of California at Berkeley and newly appointed member of the EBRPD Board, invited Bill Mott to lunch at the Athenian-Niles Club, Oakland's premier gentlemen's club.

> *I was kind of excited about it because he was the UC President, and very well thought of, and I'd gone to UC. I couldn't imagine why he invited me to lunch. It turned out that he wanted to know if I would be interested in being the general manager of the East Bay Regional Park District.*

Mott had been director of Oakland Parks Department since 1946. He told Sproul he was in the middle of completing several projects that would keep him from accepting the job for at least two years but that he would otherwise be interested. After consulting with the board, Sproul called Mott the next day and said they would wait two years if he would be willing to take the position.[222]

In the interim, the board appointed Wes Adams acting general manager. At the time of his appointment, Wes was supervisor of Redwood Park. When he was first hired in 1934, he was the sole employee of the first general manager, Elbert Vail. Adams remained a valued leader in the park district after turning over the general manager reins in 1962; he acted as the district's troubleshooter until his retirement in 1971.[223]

Mott was born in New York City and raised in Philadelphia. His father was an efficiency expert in industrial plants. Mott might not have been exposed to the wonders of nature but for the tragic death of his mother due to influenza in his senior year of high school. At the time, his dad couldn't care for three children and still do his job, so Mott was sent to live with his aunt in Jonesville, Michigan. His new high school class included only 8 students (versus the 1,500 in his school back in Philadelphia). A requirement of his class was to become a member of the 4-H program and do a farm-related project. Mott started by raising

William Penn Mott, EBRPD president. *Courtesy of EBRPD archives.*

twenty-five chickens; he won an award for the best report and was offered a scholarship to Michigan State University. He graduated from there in 1931, moved to California and completed a master's degree in landscape architecture from UC in 1933.[224]

Hired as a landscape architect and planner with the National Park Service, he went to work at the NPS Western Regional Office in San Francisco. Mott's job was to develop master plans for national parks during the winter and then to supervise the CCC work during the summer out in the field. He worked for NPS for seven years before going into private landscaping practice. He had his own office in Berkeley between 1940 and 1946 where he developed several park master plans for the City of Oakland and eventually was hired as Oakland's superintendent of parks. Mott quickly put into practice a philosophy that revolutionized park planning. "Up to that point parks were to look at but not to play in," he recalled. "I felt they could be beautiful and useful at the same time. I wanted people to stay on the grass." In 1950, he launched the highly successful Children's Fairyland at Lake Merritt. Between 1946 and 1962, he enjoyed a fifteen-year career in Oakland.[225]

PARK DISTRICT'S FOURTH MANAGER

The district board formally appointed Mott as its fourth general manager, and he assumed the position on July 1, 1962. First among the priorities, the board wanted him to "straighten out the financial programs" held over from the Walpole administration. The board also wanted him to concentrate on overall planning for the district's expansion, including consolidation, and to try to bring Contra Costa County into the EBRPD.

Mott quickly assembled a dedicated and creative headquarters staff. Among his recruits was Irwin Luckman, a local architect. Luckman would become the district's first chief of planning, design and construction. Richard Trudeau became the first chief of public relations. Chris Nelson became the first chief of interpretation, and Parry Laird was recruited as the district's first chief of parks.[226]

Mott's innovations in restructuring management offices within the park district included creating additional professional departments for finance, human resources, equipment and fire and a public safety department with sworn police officers. Mott laid the administrative foundation that was essential for the future expansion of the district. Within Tilden Regional Park, Mott created four advisory committees tasked with modernizing major features of this most developed and utilized of the eight regional parks that existed at the beginning of his tenure. These committees included a golf advisory board, the Nature Area's interpretive committee, a Botanic Garden committee and a fourth committee addressing miscellaneous matters. Each committee was tasked with exploring and investigating issues that limited the park's smooth operation.[227]

GOLF ADVISORY BOARD

In August 1962, two months after assuming his directorship, Mott announced the formation of a seven-person advisory board that included the golf course supervisor, the pro shop supervisor, the chief of parks and representatives from the men's club. Clyde de Vilbiss was appointed the committee president. Berkeley engineer Doug Stiehl, a veteran golfer, became an influential member of the committee, providing it with a hole-by-hole critique of the Tilden course. Golf course superintendent Jerry Kent became an important member of the committee starting in 1965.

The composition of the committee changed over its nine-year existence, but its objectives remained the same: to speed up play and boost revenue (see chapter 6).

NATURE AREA'S INTERPRETIVE COMMITTEE

In November 1962, Mott announced a second Tilden committee to further develop the nature education program. The interpretive committee included distinguished members of UC natural and biological science departments. The committee was chaired by Dr. Robert C. Stebbins and had representatives from both elementary education and Scout organizations. In addition to Mott and Stebbins, the interpretive committee was staffed by Chris Nelson, Jack Parker, Josh Barkin and Margaret Hutchinson (see chapter 12).

BOTANIC GARDEN COMMITTEE

In May 1964, Mott created the official Botanic Garden advisory committee, which was made up of regular visitors and others. It did not take long before the committee split into two groups: one group favored improving and enlarging the Tilden Garden, while the other wanted to relocate and expand a new native plant garden to Grass Valley Regional Park (now known as Anthony Chabot Regional Park). Each group loudly proclaimed its position in the media and before the regional park and the district board. The controversy that resulted took several twists and turns throughout the remainder of Mott's tenure (see chapter 9).

THE FOURTH COMMITTEE

The fourth committee is little remembered because its subject matter was not nearly as controversial as what occupied the attention of the other three committees. It dealt with more mundane issues such as relocating picnic areas to more central locations farther away from residential areas; rebuilding Lake Anza's concession, dressing and lifeguard buildings after the

1965 fire burned the original 1940 WPA building; dealing with opposition to the nine-hole golf course; and relocating the Golden Gate Live Steamers from Redwood Park into the new steam train complex.

In June 1964, Contra Costa County was annexed into the EBRPD, and the remaining undeveloped areas of Wildcat Canyon and a dozen other new parks were added to the regional park system (see chapter 16).

The dynamic relationship between Mott, Dr. Sproul and the EBRPD board ended early in 1967 with the resignation of Bill Mott and the retirement of Dr. Sproul. Mott left his position with the regional park district to become director of the California State Parks Department under Governor Ronald Reagan. Mott was later appointed by President Reagan to serve as the director of the National Park Service.

MANAGING VEGETATION AND OPERATING TILDEN PARK

This chapter focuses on the historic changes in the composition of vegetation, the challenges managing this vegetation and the supervisors that have taken this on.

VEGETATION CHANGES (1772–1895)

Since the first encounter between Spanish explorers and Native Americans in 1772, the area's landscape has undergone many changes to its vegetation, some natural and some man-made, on the way to becoming a regional park in 1936.

Historically, the East Bay Mediterranean climate exposed the area to coastal winds from the bay and periodic strong interior winds from the east. The region's native plant communities were repeatedly subjected to cool winter rain, dry summers, variable winds, periodic fires set by Native Americans and occasional wind-driven wildfire. As a result, the native flora was remarkably grassy, diverse and spectacular. Trees were modest in number and size and included native shrubs, oak and bay woodlands grouped in ravines and along the north and east sides of the hills.[228]

In 1797, Mission San Jose's cattle-grazing operations expanded across the East Bay hills. During the Mexican rancho era that followed until 1846, pristine native grasslands were replaced with introduced European grasses.

Upper Wildcat Canyon in 1911—Sweet Briar Dairy. *Courtesy of EBRPD archives.*

For the subsequent ninety years, grazing continued on family ranches and private watershed lands until 1936, when the park district purchased upper Wildcat Canyon.

FRANK HAVENS'S EUCALYPTUS PLANTATIONS

Tilden's abundant eucalyptus trees can be traced back to the Frank Havens stewardship of the Mahogany Eucalyptus and Land Company, formed in 1910 to grow eucalyptus for hardwood lumber. A three-thousand-acre eucalyptus plantation was developed with the intent to harvest trees, but within two decades it was apparent that the enterprise was not the gold mine it was thought to be. When the first trees planted in the East Bay in 1895 were harvested in 1913, it became clear that the wood warped easily and was impossible to mill for commercial uses. Havens's timber venture was a complete failure and was abandoned (see chapter 1).

TILDEN: A NATURAL WOODLAND

"The park will be a great natural playground for hikers, campers, picnic parties, horseback riders, and lovers of nature," explained Ansel Hall of the National Park Service, in the Olmsted/Hall Proposed Parkland Plan. "It will be a park in the sense that Yosemite and Yellowstore are parks, not a city park to be admired only for its beauty, but a great natural woodland area to provide recreation for thousands of citizens who cannot afford to go to national parks, or even to Santa Cruz or Marin county."

Natural woodland or not, between 1937 and 1941, the district used CCC and WPA workers to plant redwood and other trees under the direction of landscape architect Arthur B. Hyde and Botanic Garden director Jim Roof (with consultation from Howard McMinn and John McLaren). They planted Monterey pine, oak, redwood, giant sequoia, elm, willow and poplar trees; manzanita, buckeye, greasewood, coffeeberry and other shrubs; iris, fern and a huge variety of other flowers and bushes. All were considered for impact on soil conservation and value in creating park-like ground cover. Unfortunately, the advent of World War II resulted in the loss of the large, inexpensive workforce and ended organized planting projects at Tilden.

The park district implemented planting programs over the next twenty-five years, adding groves of Monterey pine to Tilden's eucalyptus forests and grassy hillsides. Jim Roof continued to direct this planting project. He despised the eucalyptus trees that Havens had planted and, in later years, deeply regretted having overseen the planting of Monterey pine and other species in the park's grasslands, which had replaced the once amazing displays of spring wildflowers.[229]

From the mid-1940s through the 1960s, the district operated Tilden with a small crew of park employees. These crews were focused on developing public-use areas and park operations and were not able to improve or maintain the natural or man-made vegetation in the park's 1,729 acres of open space (83 percent of the park). For most of its existence, the land management philosophy of the EBRPD had been to "let nature take its course" without intervention or expenditure of significant park funds. The distinction between native and nonnative vegetation was not of major concern for the earliest park managers or even the public who enjoyed Tilden.

During the 1970s and '80s, the district increased its staffing and became more professional, using resource specialists who applied science-based

Aerial view of Wildcat Canyon looking north, 1935. Note the extensive grasslands along the proposed park's eastern ridge and eucalyptus groves in the center valley and western ridge. *Courtesy of EBRPD archives.*

management policies and environmental planning principles. District staff sought assistance from state agencies to provide funding in order to prepare the 1988 Tilden Land Use Plan (LUP) and Environment Impact Report (EIR).

TILDEN VEGETATION TODAY:
A COMPLEX MIXTURE

After its many years as grassland for cattle grazing, few remnants of wildflower species, shrubs and trees remained when Tilden was shaped into a large regional park. Among those native species that did survive were California poppies, Pacific coast irises, coast live oaks and California bay laurel trees. What grows in the park now reflects a complex intermingling of native and nonnative species surviving in a variety of unique habitats. Ultimately, the park's vegetation is a botanical hodgepodge of planted exotics and native species.

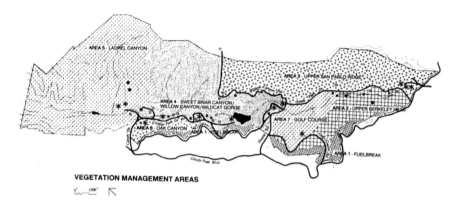

1988 Environmental Impact Report, Tilden Park Vegetation Management Areas. *Courtesy of EBRPD archives.*

The 1988 Plan and Report divided Tilden Park into seven major areas that include all of the park's 1,805 acres of vegetation and open space. The report, as follows, described the typical vegetation and features found in these management areas and recommended policies for improving wildlife habitat and for protecting special species of plants.

Area 1: Ridgetop Fuelbreak

This 150-acre area was established in 1973 as part of the emergency work following the 1972 freeze. Eucalyptus trees were removed and the area between Golf Gate Road and Canon Drive was converted to a maintained grassy area where a fire originating within the Park might be stopped before reaching adjacent urban areas.

Park Policies and Required Actions: maintain fuelbreak area, but restore natural screening provided adjacent residential areas by former vegetation. Provide screen plantings along portions of Wildcat Canyon Road, with willow or redwood plantings in moist swales.

Area 2: Upper Berkeley Hills

This 160-acre area is a rich mixture of north-facing moist shrubland and woodland. Patches of eucalyptus totaling about 40 acres were removed in 1974 after the freeze of 1972. The eucalyptus stumps have since resprouted. In the north section, native oak, bay, and shrubland with woodland trees blend with the Frowning Ridge Fuelbreak and the redwoods at Gillespie Camp and the Steam Train redwoods at Southgate.

Park Policies and Required Actions: Foster indigenous shrub and tree establishment within and around existing eucalyptus stands and allow the replacement of non-indigenous shrub and trees in areas where indigenous vegetation exhibits healthy growth.

Area 3: Upper San Pablo Ridge

This 500-acre area includes the west-facing grassland slope along San Pablo Ridge below the Sea View Trail. The vegetation is predominantly grassland that is prime Alameda whipsnake habitat. Encroaching pine and eucalyptus trees planted in the '40s or coppiced from eucalyptus removed in the mid-'70s dot the area's slopes. In the South around Vollmer Peak, groves of planted pine, eucalyptus, native shrubs, and oak/bay woodland reach down to South Park Drive. In the North planted pine and eucalyptus crown the ridge and border Wildcat Road, leaving the center as disturbed grassland where the abandoned nine-hole golf course was graded.

Park Policies and Required Action: Maintain the existing grass-brushland through prescribed burning: pine and eucalyptus stands by occasional thinning. No further plantings of either pine or eucalyptus. Promote indigenous vegetation on Vollmer Peak.

Area 4: Sweetbrier Canyon and Wildcat Gorge

This 275-acre area is predominantly grassland with large stands of coyote brush. Dry slopes are dominated by dense shrub land. Its moist slopes and riparian stream areas, willow groves, big leaf maple, and oak/bay woodland provide areas of relief and shade.

Park Policies and Required Actions: Maintain and increase existing grasslands by mechanical means and/or prescribed burnings. Remove the forest litter in eucalyptus groves to prevent major wildfires. Remove artichoke thistles and coyote brush.

Area 5: Laurel Canyon

This 550-acre site includes the Tilden Nature Area and two large blue gum eucalyptus forests that overtop the riparian vegetation along Wildcat Creek. Shrub land and oak woodland dominate the east-facing dry slopes, while the Nike grove of blue gum eucalyptus and the Rotary grove of sequoia big trees are on the ridge near Wildcat Peak. The moist East-facing slopes above Wildcat Creek are covered with willow, bays, and north coastal shrub land.

Park Policies and Required Actions: Maintain and enhance the existing indigenous landscape through gradual vegetation changes where appropriate. Prevent the spread of young eucalyptus, with occasional thinning within the groves. Remove litter accumulations through hand picking and/or prescribed fire. Maintain grassland on the south and southwest slopes. Prohibit new plantings to allow for natural regeneration of indigenous vegetation.

Area 6: Oak Canyon

This 50-acre area includes the north-facing slopes with oak, bay and willow woodland below Wildcat Canyon Road, bounded by Central Park Drive and Canon Drive. Numerous landslides dot the moist slopes that support riparian flora, shrubs, and trees.

Park Policies and Required Actions: Protect mature indigenous trees. Remove exotic plants which are adversely affecting indigenous growth. Thin young eucalyptus along Canon Drive to benefit oak understory. Remove broom and German ivy.

Area 7: Golf Course

This area includes the 120-acre Tilden Golf Course.

Park Policies and Required Actions: Park negotiated with American Golf to develop a program for controlling the potential movement of chemicals into Wildcat Creek. The creek restoration was completed in 2013 (see chapter 6).

KNOWN WILDFIRE RISKS

Ever since Tilden Park was established, memories of the 1923 Berkeley firestorm were a constant reminder to the district's directors and staff of their dual responsibility of providing the public with opportunities for their enjoyment of the park's natural and recreational attributes while protecting them from another catastrophe. Aging trees (especially Monterey pines planted in the early 1900s), vulnerable grasses and shrubs are a normal element of wildfire risk that needs to be controlled.

The park is also subject to risks associated with abnormal and changing weather patterns:

- Drought conditions appear to be more common due to global warming;
- Tilden's last freeze in 1972 killed or damaged most ridge top eucalyptus trees;
- Diablo winds from the northeast occur every fall between September and November. These high fire danger conditions are labeled "red flag days" by the National Weather Service.

Virtually all the development in the East Bay hills occurred during a seventy-year period when agencies and homeowners did not understand or respect the potential wildfire danger created by diablo winds. As a consequence, the pattern of residential development combined with the hills' unique natural features had increased the potential for home loss.

1991 OAKLAND HILLS FIRESTORM

The 1991 conflagration is known as the Oakland Hills Firestorm. The fire ultimately killed 25 people and injured 150 others. Some 1,520 acres were destroyed, including 2,843 single-family dwellings and 437 apartment and condominium units. The economic loss was estimated at $1.5 billion. The blaze that originated south of Tilden caused a shift in public understanding of extreme wildfire behavior in the hills. It expanded the focus of government oversight from local and regional to state and federal sponsorship of hazard reduction programs.

2010 WILDFIRE HAZARD REDUCTION PROGRAM

This program covered all the hill parks between Lake Chabot and Wildcat Canyon.[230] A state-sponsored environmental plan (EIR) recommended *thinning mature eucalyptus forests to a 20 to 25 foot spacing (100 trees per acre) for medium sized trees, and 30 foot spacing (50 trees per acre) for larger trees. Thinning groves then requires ongoing pruning and removal of sprouts, and understory every 3 to 5 years to create a maintained forest with a rather bare understory.*

Over the last seven years, the East Bay Regional Park District has spent over $6.6 million on removing dead or seedling trees in the East Bay hills to protect surrounding communities. Much of the work has been funded by Measure CC, a $12-per-acre parcel tax.[231]

2015 FEMA HAZARD REDUCTION AND RESOURCE MANAGEMENT PLAN

The Federal Emergency Management Agency (FEMA), an agency of the Department of Homeland Security, has provided additional disaster avoidance research funding. The federally sponsored environmental report made virtually the same recommendations as the state-sponsored 2010 EIR evaluation mentioned earlier. In 2015, the park board accepted $4.65 million in FEMA funding to continue its hazard reduction program, selectively removing or thinning nonnative trees and brush in eleven regional parks, including Tilden Regional Park.[232]

The district recently awarded a contract for $377,000 to thin thirty-four acres and remove twenty-nine hazardous blue gum eucalyptus at $3,000 per tree. Operation staff's current estimate is $8,000 per acre for the initial effort and $1,000 per year for annual maintenance. The estimated cost projection for Tilden Park is approximately $15 million over the next twenty years.[233]

WHO MANAGES TILDEN PARK'S VEGETATION?

The district has been organized to use employees, contractors, concessionaires and volunteers, all in a seamless manner. Tilden is directly managed by a park supervisor, a supervising naturalist and a Botanic Garden director, each with employees for their assigned areas.

Public safety provides police, fire and lifeguard services; trades provide skilled craft services; and the administrative departments of the East Bay Regional Park District headquarters in Oakland provide a full range of office support services.

PUBLIC ATTRACTIONS MAINTAINED
BY TILDEN PARK CREWS

PICNICKING: There are a dozen reservable picnic areas in Tilden Park. There are barbecues at most picnic areas. Trails and picnic areas remain open year-round.

WEDDINGS AND RECEPTIONS: Weddings and receptions in Tilden Park may be held at three reservable picnic areas in addition to the Botanic Garden and the Brazilian Room.

SWIMMING. Lake Anza is jointly operated by Tilden Park's crew and the public safety lifeguards. The sandy beach is open to the sun and sheltered from the wind, with lifeguards posted during the swim season. Picnic grounds are located nearby. Swim season is normally May through September.

FISHING. Lake Anza is open for fishing year-round. The lake is not stocked but has naturally occurring largemouth bass, bluegill, sunfish and channel catfish. A state fishing license is required for anglers aged sixteen or older.

GROUP CAMPING. Camping facilities for organized groups are in four locations.

TRAILS. The maintenance of the 39.41 miles of equestrian, hiking and biking trails in Tilden Park is the joint responsibility of park crews and volunteers (see chapter 5).

CONCESSIONS. Tilden's concessions include the Lake Anza Beach Café, merry-go-round, steam trains and the golf course. Park supervisor ensures that the concessionaires and the district are adhering to the concession operating agreements.

TILDEN PARK SUPERVISORS SINCE 1985

Rachel McDonald, Supervisor between 1985 and 1990

Hired by the district in 1974, she worked on road and trail crews in several parks and as Redwood Park supervisor for four years before coming to Tilden Park in 1985. She was one of a group of women hired into field positions when the park district was under court order to have a more diverse workforce. McDonald brought her own style of supervision, creating an atmosphere of fun mixed with accountability.

> *During my time at Tilden, the job of Park Supervisor evolved. Initially, the job was more like a lead person, but over time it became a much more professional position because I needed to know more about a range of topics, from natural resources management; labor relations; contract administration; to risk management. The liaison work at Tilden Park was more complex than other parks because of its size, the many ways it is used, the number agencies and parks surrounding Tilden, and the residential neighbors who keep an eye on the park.*

McDonald was promoted to unit manager of regional trails in 1990 and later to the Parklands unit, which includes Tilden. She retired in 2005 and described her years at Tilden as "one of the happiest times of my life."[234]

Jeff Wilson, Supervisor from 1990 to 2005

Wilson was hired in 1974 as part of the new wave of college graduates that followed the adoption of the EBRPD 1973 master plan, which projected a doubling of parklands. Jeff worked in several parks as a ranger, advanced to supervisor of Wildcat Canyon and then supervised Tilden Park for fifteen years. Heading up such a heavily used park meant learning lessons in public relations and politics. He then put all those skills to use as the district's "Wild lands" unit manager, overseeing all the large open space parks before being promoted to chief of park operations in 2010. He retired two years later, in 2012. "I stayed at the park district for so long in part because it was like a big family," says Wilson. "In the end, it was more about people than parks."[235]

Davio Santos, Supervisor from 2005 to 2010

Davio began his career at the park district as a park ranger at Contra Loma in 1977. In 1990, he was promoted to park supervisor at Wildcat Canyon Regional Park, where he worked for fifteen years until he became supervisor of Tilden Park. In addition to managing a very busy park, he worked to improve the park's fuel break program and installed an all-accessible picnic area. He oversaw the installation of glass doors that surround the merry-go-round ride and introduced a native garden to the lawn area adjacent to the parking lot at the carousel. He took over maintenance duties for the group camps, Wildcat View, New Woodland and Blue Gum. In 2010, Davio became the district's Delta unit manager, responsible for Briones, the Alameda and Contra Costa Alternative Work Programs, eighty-eight miles of regional trails and Big Break, Carquinez and Martinez Regional Shorelines before retiring in 2014.[236]

Sergio Huerta, Supervisor since 2010

In 1989, he attended Skyline City College, where he enrolled in the California Conservation Corps on campus after seeing an advertisement for a job that promised hard work with low pay, constructing and maintaining trails, fighting fires and working on a variety of natural resource projects.

Sergio's career at the park district began with a six-month temporary position at Tilden working for Rachel McDonald, followed in 1991 by a ranger position on roads and trails that lasted for thirteen years. He was promoted to park craft specialist in Anthony Chabot Regional Park in 2005 and remained there for almost three years. In 2008, he was promoted to park supervisor of the East County Regional Trail system, Vasco Caves, Bay Point Regional Shoreline, Antioch Pier and the expanding Big Break Regional Park.

Sergio Huerta, current Tilden Park supervisor. *Photo by Jerry Kent, retired EBRPD assistant general manager.*

Sergio commented after he was made Tilden Park supervisor in 2010: "It gives me immense pride, honor and humility as I learn on the job from the people I work with at Tilden. I begin every day at Tilden thinking about how we can improve this park's ever-changing landscape while serving the public at this grand old park."[237]

TILDEN PARK AND THE EAST BAY REGIONAL PARK DISTRICT TODAY

W hen Tilden opened in 1937, the population of the East Bay was about 400,000. Census figures reported 1.5 million residents living in Alameda and Contra Costa Counties by 1960. The population had quadrupled in just two decades, yet the number of regional parks had not increased. The district's 1934 property tax cap limited regional park fees, even though the district had expanded into southern Alameda County in 1958 and into Contra Costa County in 1964 as it moved toward becoming a two-county regional park agency.

William Penn Mott Jr., then superintendent of Oakland parks, agreed to become general manager in 1962, and he would guide the park district into the future. In 1963, the state's legislature and Governor Edmund "Pat" Brown updated the district's authority to double its property tax fees to acquire, develop and operate new parks. As a result, eighteen new parks were acquired between 1961 and 1974 for a total of twenty-four regional parks. Population had quadrupled, and now the number of regional parks had done so as well.

An energized EBRPD led by Mott and Richard Trudeau, Mott's successor in 1968, quickly acquired and began developing the new parks, to be opened soon after acquisition. By 1970, the 1930 Olmsted/Hall Plan was finally realized. Tilden became part of an extensive ten-park system that formed a nearly continuous twenty-six-mile-long chain of parks from Lake Chabot to Wildcat Canyon, a whopping thirteen thousand total acres of parklands in the hilltops behind the district's founding seven cities. It was no longer necessary for Tilden to be the "one and all" park for area residents. Recreational facilities and park features could now be spread throughout a much larger system of regional parks, and the expanding East Bay population had many choices for finding recreational opportunities in nature.

Proposition 13 and the California taxpayers' revolt of 1978 sent a message to all public agencies, including the EBRPD. Acquisitions were slowed until revenues and grants made it possible to add new parks and trails. During the nineteen-year period between 1968 and 1987, the district was able to add thirty-three new regional parks and sixteen new regional trails and preserve forty-three thousand acres of the East Bay's most scenic parklands. This was a time of challenge as well as a critical period for acquiring new parklands to keep up with urban growth.

In 1985, Richard Trudeau retired. Pat O'Brien became general manager in 1988, and district voters approved the passage of Measure AA, a $225 million bond to provide funding for both regional and local park projects. In 1992, the rest of Murray Township (Livermore Area) was annexed with appropriate changes made to the district's master plan to now cover all of Alameda and Contra Costa Counties. Measure AA was implemented over a twenty-year period, allowing Pat O'Brien, future general manager Robert Doyle and the board to add fifteen new regional parks and fifteen new regional trails and preserve thirty-four thousand additional acres.

California passed measure WW in 2008 to extend Measure AA for an additional twenty years. Ironically, Measure WW's 71.92 percent approval rating was roughly the same percentage rate as the original ballot measure in 1934 that created the East Bay Regional Park District. Measure CC has provided funding for park access, wildfire protection, public safety and environmental maintenance projects within the East Bay Regional Parks since 2004. Voters in western Alameda and Contra Costa Counties overwhelmingly passed Measure FF in November 2018 with 85.6 percent of the vote, extending Measure CC funding for an additional fifteen years.

In 2011, Pat O'Brien retired, and Robert Doyle was selected by the board to be the next district general manager, culminating his forty-year career in park district service that included twenty-four years managing land acquisitions.

Today, Tilden is one of 73 regional parks with a combined 121,397 acres, a chain of 1,250 miles of trails and parklands that are spread throughout Alameda and Contra Costa Counties. The East Bay Regional Park District is the largest regional park agency in the country, hosting twenty-five million visitors annually.

Board of directors, 2018. *Pictured here are, from left to right*: Whitney Dotson, Ayn Wieskamp, Beverly Lane, Robert E. Doyle (*standing*), Dennis Waspi, Dee Rosario, Ellen Corbett and Colin Coffey. *Courtesy of EBRPD archives.*

While much has been accomplished over the past eighty-five years, there is a lot more to do. Tilden Regional Park and the East Bay Regional Park District will always remain works in progress, as the district continues to provide regional parks and trails that are not only desired but also vitally necessary for the quality of life of East Bay residents as the population approaches three million.

Despite the rapid expansion of the regional park system, Tilden Park, due to its history, location, size and diversity of attractions, still draws nearly one million annual visitors and retains the title of "Queen of the Regional Parks."[238]

NOTES

Introduction

1. Beverly R. Ortiz, "Ohlone Curriculum with Bay Miwok Content and Introduction to Delta Yokuts," East Bay Regional Park District [hereafter EBRPD], 2015, www.ebparks.org/civicax/filebank/blobdload.aspx?BlobID=22874, 14–17, 39–43; Beverly R. Ortiz, "Student Resources: Bay Miwok Content," EBRPD, https://www.ebparks.org/civicax/filebank/blobdload.aspx?BlobID=22877, 3–7, 10–11; Randall Milliken, *A Time of Little Choice: The Disintegration of Tribal Culture in the San Francisco Bay Area, 1769–1810* (Menlo Park, CA: Malki Museum, 2009), 21–26, 33, 36–37, 55–56, 137–62, 228–29, 233, 243.
2. Neil Havelik, "Charles Lee Tilden Regional Park," a resource analysis prepared for the EBRPD in January 1975, 3.
3. Wikipedia, "Rancho El Sobrante," last modified June 13, 2018, https://en.wikipedia.org/wiki/Rancho_El_Sobrante.
4. Treaty with Mexico (February 2, 1848), www.azteca.net/aztec/guadhida.html.
5. Wikipedia, "Ranchos of California," last modified January 27, 2019, https://en.wikipedia.org/wiki/Ranchos_of_California.
6. "Years of Litigation for Rancho Sobrante," *Oakland Tribune*, March 10, 1909.
7. Havelik, "Charles Lee Tilden Regional Park," 4–6.
8. Randall Milliken, Laurence H. Shoup and Beverly R. Ortiz, "Ohlone/Costanoan Indians of the San Francisco Peninsula and Their Neighbors, Yesterday and Today," Muwekma Ohlone Tribe of the San Francisco Bay

Area, http://www.muwekma.org/images/Ohlone_Costanoan_Indians_
of_SF_Peninsula_NPS_2009.pdf, 175–76.

Chapter 1

9. John Wesley Noble, *Its Name Was M.U.D.: A Story of Water* (Oakland, CA: EBMUD, 1970), 3, describes the April 1858 legislation.
10. Noble, *Its Name Was M.U.D.*, identifies (162) seven private water companies that were directly absorbed into the CCWC and five others that were absorbed into one of those seven companies. This list excludes other companies that acquired water lands but never produced a drop of water.
11. Havens's partnership with Borax Smith lasted until 1910, when the partners decided to split their assets, valued at $2 million each, with Smith taking the transportation companies and Havens taking the water and real estate companies
12. *Berkeley Gazette*, November 11, 1920 editorial.
13. Havelik, "Charles Lee Tilden Regional Park," 7.
14. Noble, *Its Name Was M.U.D.*
15. "George Pardee: 1903–1907," Governors' Gallery, http://governors. library.ca.gov/21-Pardee.html; "George Pardee," Wikipedia, last modified September 28, 2018, https://en.wikipedia.org/wiki/George_Pardee.
16. The low water reserves were due to a combination of increased demand caused by population and industrial growth and periodic drought conditions. Ninety years later in 2019, California finds itself in a statewide drought situation without resolution.
17. *Oakland Tribune*, October 20, 1929.
18. Ibid.
19. *Oakland Tribune*, January 5, 1930. Headwaters Power Project is described as due to be completed in 1934 and expected to generate 228,000 horsepower.

Chapter 2

20. In 1906, Oakland's city planner Charles Mulford Robinson urged the creation of parklands in the hills, and Dr. Werner Hegemann, another Oakland city planner, called for parklands along the shore, within the city and in the hills in 1915.

21. Wikipedia, "Joseph Leconte," last modified December 31, 2018, https://en.wikipedia.org/wiki/Joseph_LeConte. Formed in 1892 and based on a similar eastern club, the Appalachian Mountain Club. Among others included in early planning of the club was UC professor of geology and early conservationist Joseph LeConte.

22. French joined the Sierra Club in 1908 and served on its local walks committee for ten years before founding the Contra Costa Hiking Club on February 22, 1920. He credited John Muir as his inspiration for founding the club.

23. Harold French's biographical information is a combination of quotes from a one-page "Harold French Biography" July 7, 2012, by Amelia Marshall (EBRPD), a sketch of him in the Monty Monteagle papers (EBRPD archives) and Jack Burroughs, "This Is the Story of Your Town," *Oakland Tribune*, May 18, 1948.

24. *Oakland Tribune*, September 18, 1923.

25. "New Scenic Road Opens in Berkeley," *Oakland Tribune*, August 22, 1932.

26. *Oakland Tribune*, January 8, 1929.

27. The cause of the rift between Davis and Pardee is supposition based on the proximity of the release of Davis's letters and his resignation. Davis sent "informal letters of inquiry" to the Oakland and Berkeley park departments on January 8, 1929. A Berkeley ballot measure was announced in March, the first regional parks campaign organization was announced in April and Davis's resignation was announced on May 6, 1929. It may have been he was just ready to move on to the next project. Arthur P. Davis announced his retirement from EBMUD in May 1929 and took a two-year assignment as an advisory engineer for the Soviet Union focusing on hydroelectric dam projects for Turkistan.

28. *Oakland Tribune*, January 11, 1929.

29. The month before (December 1928), EBMUD had agreed to pay $35 million for acquisition of the East Bay Water Company's distribution system after receiving $26 million from the government for the purchase. The extra $9 million of debt was no doubt the motivation behind selling unneeded properties

30. The city originally planned to purchase 1,400 acres, but the utility district's price was too high to justify the acquisition. The $350,000 bond measure proposed a 700-acre Wildcat Canyon park from Grizzly Peak in the north to the caves, including the old Bruno Ranch.

31. The day before the election, more than 4,000 Berkeleyans visited the site of the proposed park in a community-sponsored "open house." Forty

telephone workers were employed to get out the vote, but of the 47,000 registered voters, only 10,887 went to the polls.

32. Summaries of Professor May's career from University of California, Berkeley Bancroft Library and EBRPD archives.

33. Ansel Hall to Samuel May, "On the Survey for the Proposed East Bay Forest Park," May 13, 1930.

34. During 1928, Olmsted and his staff visited more than 1,000 sites and recommended 125 scenic places for preservation as state parks, after which he was said to have collapsed from the effort of completing the survey. Note: In a February 20, 1929 memo to the California State Parks commission, Olmsted note his exclusion of the Contra Costa Hills Park from consideration as a state park due to the property's high urban values and his preference for properties clearly within municipal government jurisdiction. (I interpreted this as his recommendation for the formation of the future East Bay Regional Park District.)

35. George Gibbs Jr. worked for the Olmsted Brothers firm for a total of thirty-two years, first in the home office in Brookline, Massachusetts, then in an office in Palos Verdes, California, managing West Coast projects.

36. "Park Survey First Project of Kahn Fund," *San Francisco Chronicle*, January 25, 1931.

37. For the current status of the Bay Ridge Trail, go to www.ridgetrail.org.

38. Harland Frederick quotations from the foreword to 1984 reprint of the 1930 "Olmsted-Hall Report."

39. "Hearing Set on Contra Costa Hills Park Site," *Oakland Tribune*, September 19,1934.

40. The 1964 annexation did not include Liberty Union School District (East of Antioch to the county line—Oakley and Brentwood area). It was annexed in 1981.

41. When Contra Costa County withdrew from the campaign in June 1934, representatives from the cities of El Cerrito, Emeryville and Richmond resigned from the board.

42. Wikipedia, "Robert Gordon Sproul," last modified November 28, 2018, https://en.wikipedia.org/wiki/Robert_Gordon_Sproul.

43. "Only 5,000 Signatures Were Required to Advance the Legislation," *Oakland Tribune*, August 11, 1933.

44. *Olmsted Hall Report*, 1984 reprint, reference from foreword.

45. "The November 4th Open House Included a Hike Led by the Contra Costa Hiking Club," *Oakland Tribune*, November 2, 1934.

46. SERA was California's version of the Works Progress Administration and provided government-sponsored projects for unemployed men during the Depression. After WPA legislation was passed in 1935, SERA projects were absorbed into the WPA; "Regional Park Fete Planned," *Oakland Tribune*, November 2, 1934.

47. A June 5, 1935 letter from J.S. Longwell, chief engineer and general manager, to Leroy Goodrich, EBRPD director, delineates the 6,261 acres of EBMUD property offered for a price of $2,179,823.

48. Thomas J. Roberts letter citing independent land valuation, January 16, 1936.

49. Elbert Vail, *The Early Story of the East Bay Regional Parks*, EBRPD, 5.

50. Letter to seven East Bay mayors dated November 15, 1935, from EBRPD board signed by T.J. Roberts.

51. Final terms reported in June 11, 1936 newspapers, including *Piedmonter* and *Roosevelt News*.

52. The sixty-six acres known as Redwood Bowl was purchased for the park district on January 3, 1936—the first land acquired by the regional park district. It was acquired from the McNee family estate for $2,130 with funds advanced by Major Tilden. The Redwood Bowl was incorporated into Redwood Regional Park along with several other private land acquisitions between 1938 and 1939. In 1952, the eighty-two-acre Roberts Regional Park was acquired and developed adjacent to Redwood Regional Park. Roberts Park was eventually expanded in the 1970s when Redwood Bowl and the Redwood archery area were transferred from Redwood to Roberts for operational purposes.

53. *Oakland Tribune*, October 19, 1936.

54. Other newspapers reported that Mayor William J. McCracken of Oakland, Mayor Edward M. Ament of Berkeley and Major James Eschen of Alameda also spoke.

55. *Berkeley Gazette*, July 17, 1936.

Chapter 3

56. In the 1860s, the Russian engineer acquired land and water surrounding the Truckee River and formed the Lake Tahoe and San Francisco Water Company to export water to San Francisco, but he was outmaneuvered by Nevada dam builders. He supervised the construction of the Spring Valley water system (Nilda Rego, "Days

Gone By: In 1865, Alexis Waldemar Von Schmidt Schemes to Provide San Francisco with Water," *Contra Costa Times*, June 15, 2014). Schmidt built the Hunters Point Dry docks where clipper ships were serviced and was lauded for removing the "unmovable" Blossom Rock, long a navigation menace in San Francisco Bay.

57. C.N. Alexander, "A Truly Colorful Career, Major Tilden Will BE Feted on 90th Birthday," *Oakland Post Enquirer*, July 18, 1947, summarizes Major Tilden's life milestones.

58. Vollmer was appointed professor of police administration in UC's political science department.

59. Founding board site names: Vollmer Peak, Tilden Park, Reinhardt Grove (Redwood Park) and Roberts Park; Goodrich was the exception, said to be due to his long tenure, by which time honoring past directors this way was considered passé.

60. The award was named after Benjamin Wheeler, a former president of the university, and was awarded biannually by the Berkeley Service Clubs Council. Emery was also a councilor of the University of California Alumni Association

61. *Oakland Tribune*, October 4, 1902.

62. "Campaign Launched to Raise $400,000 in Eastbay for Mills College Fund," *Oakland Tribune*, February 17, 1923.

63. Clare B. Fischer, "Aurelia Henry Reinhardt: President of Mills College 1877–1948," one-page summary provided by Mills College.

Chapter 4

64. This War Department cabinet position nowadays is known as the secretary of defense.

65. The 1933 wages converted to 2011 unskilled wages using MeasuringWorth.com, a service for calculating relative worth over time.

66. "Ansel Hall, Pioneer Interpreter," *Courier* 4, no. 7 (August 1981).

67. *Berkeley Daily Guardian*, April 12, 1937.

68. Company 5446 work record was delineated in the *Official Annual Guide of the Sacramento District Ninth Corp Area of the Civilian Conservation Corps for 1938*, courtesy of EBRPD archives.

69. "CCC Camp Wildcat Camp to Close," *Oakland Tribune*, April 27, 1941, reported the composition of the last CCC company at Tilden Park. The article concluded with "during the winter [of 1940] the boys have done

much work in the region in and around Tilden Park golf course, part of the Regional Park system."

70. Wildcat Canyon camp newspapers were provided by the Center for Research Libraries, University of Chicago. The October 1938 issue of the *Wildcat* was produced by Company 5446.

71. Charles A. Birnbaum and Lisa Crowder, eds., *Pioneers of American Landscape Design, an Annotated Bibliography* (Washington, D.C.: U.S. Department of the Interior, National Park Service, Cultural Resources, Preservation Assistance Division, Historic Landscape Initiative, 1993), 51.

72. Alan Kaplan, "The Civilian Conservation Corps Formed 70 Years Ago Built EBRPD," EBRPD Nature Area, 2004.

73. Vollmer's credentials are covered in chapter 3; letter from park board to Mr. A.D. Wilder, PWA director for Northern California, dated April 25, 1935.

74. Treasure Island is an artificial island built by the federal government for the Golden Gate International Exposition (GGIE). The exposition was open from February through October 1939 and May through September 1940. FDR addressed the crowd via radio during opening ceremonies, showcasing the goods of nations bordering the Pacific Ocean. The Bay Bridge was opened in 1936 and the Golden Gate Bridge in 1937.

75. Western Union telegram, May 24, 1935.

76. A five-page WPA Form 301 was filed for project no. 0803-127. (A copy of the proposal is in the EBRPD archives.)

77. "East Bay Regional Park Projects OK'd," *Courier*, October 26,1935.

78. *Berkeley Daily Gazette*, November 2, 1936. Democratic congressman Tolan was reelected six times, serving twelve years representing the Seventh Congressional District.

79. "Construction of New Scenic Road Has Begun," *Oakland Tribune*, October 22, 1935. Local sponsors of WPA grants were responsible for a small portion of project costs satisfied by the loan of equipment and materials.

80. "Men at Work Building in the East Bay Park Area," *Oakland Tribune*, January 12, 1936.

81. "Benefits to East Bay from WPA Projects," *Roosevelt News*, May 28, 1936.

82. "Regional Park Land Is Secured," *Albany Enterprise*, June 11, 1936.

83. "2000 Trees for Hill Park Arrive," *Berkeley Daily Guardian*, March 1,1937.

84. OPS 465-03-2-53, provided by the National Archives and Records Administration, Pacific Region, San Bruno, California.

85. "$1,075,551 Grant Starts Regional Park Program," *Oakland Tribune*, May 5, 1938.

86. Grant from Federal Emergency Administration of Public Works, May 20,1938, to Elbert Vail courtesy of EBRPD archives.

87. Vail's 1939 Annual Report identified twenty-two major projects completed, EBRPD archives.

88. "50,000 Trees Soon to Be Planted in Regional Park," *Berkeley Daily Guardian*, January 20, 1940.

89. OPS 165-1-08-52, provided by the National Archives and Records Administration, Pacific Region, San Bruno, California.

90. "Vail Resigns as Regional Park Chief, Offers Service to U.S.," *Oakland Tribune*, January 15, 1942.

91. "Parks Need Little Money," *Oakland Tribune*, March 23, 1942.

Chapter 5

92. Hal Johnson, "So We Are Told," *Berkeley Daily Gazette*, November 3, 1949. Johnson's column on Curran farm history.

93. EBRPD report, July 16, 1936.

94. Amelia Sue Marshall and Terry Tobey, *Oakland's Equestrian Heritage* (Charleston, SC: Arcadia Publishing, 2008).

95. According to the CSHA history on the club's website, https://californiastatehorsemen.org.

96. Valerie J. Nelson, "George Cardinet Jr., 97; Father of State and Federal Trails Systems," *Los Angeles Times*, January 31, 2007.

97. George Cardinet, oral history, 1982, EBRPD archives.

98. The 1972 EBRPD Two County Regional Trail Plan specified: "The District will acquire, develop, and operate a Regional Trail System with the overall objective of providing a comprehensive system of trails both through and connecting its parklands with each other and with other trail systems."

99. EBRPD Master Plan, December 4, 1973, part III, p. 31, "Recreation Policies."

100. Devin Binder, MD, is a neurosurgeon based in Orange County and a medical professor at the University of California, Riverside. He vividly remembers spotting the "No Horses" sign in 1974—the incident that launched the formation of the TWHA.

101. Founders of the Tilden-Wildcat Association were Jane Binder, Lucile Arnon, Debby Young, Es Anderson and her husband, Jock Anderson.

102. www.ebparks.org/activities/biking/mountain and www.bayarearides.com/rides/tilden, as well as several other mountain bike websites, offer

mountain bikers suggestions as to trails along the Tilden-Wildcat corridor available for their use.

103. Volunteer Hiking Patrol charter members included Henry and Susan Losee, the Olrich family, Bill King of the Berkeley Hiking Club, Joe Goldstein and Tom and Doris Martin. King was elected the first chair of the group.

Chapter 6

104. "East Bay Regional Golf Course Now Open," *Oakland Tribune*, November 7, 1937, reference to Roy Butler's idea for Berkeley golf course.

105. Dewey Longworth was a former professional golfer who had played alongside Walter Hagen and Bobby Jones and held the course record at his home course with a 62.

106. "Golf Course in Wildcat Canyon Hinges on Deal," *Berkeley Daily Gazette*, January 4, 1936.

107. In 1936, Alameda County golf courses included (public) Lake Chabot Golf Course (Oakland, 1923) and Chuck Corica–North Course (Alameda, 1927); (private) Claremont Country Club (Oakland, 1903), Sequoyah Country Club (Oakland, 1913) and Castlewood Country Club (Pleasanton, 1927).

108. Billy Bell–designed courses include the Stanford University course, Chuck Corica (North) and Castlewood Country Club (Hills Course) in Northern California and Torrey Pines and Los Angeles Country Club in Southern California. The Bells also designed courses in Arizona, Nevada, Utah, Idaho, Oregon, Wisconsin, Hawaii and Mexico.

109. Richard Walpole, "Construction of the Tilden Regional Park Golf Course" *Golfdom, the Business Journal of Golf*, February 1938.

110. This was one of several excerpts from the "The Diary of Richard Walpole 1937–39," transcribed by Richard Langs for the EBRPD archives, from the diary provided by Walpole's daughter, Mary Granen.

111. Art Rosenblum, "New Links Open Amid Ohs and Ahs," *San Francisco Chronicle*, November 8, 1937.

112. "Tilden Park Preview Held," *Berkeley Daily Gazette*, November 8, 1937.

113. *San Francisco Examiner (East Bay Edition)*, November 11, 1936, American Legion dedication ceremony.

114. The Ingleside Golf Course was later renamed the San Francisco Golf Club.

115. "Of the Golfer's Friend," *Berkeley Daily Gazette*, April 14,1961, Bert Johnson reference.

116. "C.L. Warren, Women's Club's First President," *Oakland Tribune*, May 6, 1938.

117. Taken from the Tilden Women's Golf Club website, tildenwomensgolf. org.

118. Based on EBRPD news releases dated August 16, 1966. and September 16, 1966.

119. *Oakland Tribune*, April 15, 1966

120. EBRPD Board minutes, June 18,1968

121. *Oakland Tribune*, June 25, 1970.

122. Quote from author's conversation with Jerry Kent.

123. District fact sheet provides the background of Sandy's team. Don Morrison had seven and a half years' experience as the golf pro at Culver Greens in Culver City and was then the teaching pro at Westchester Golf Course in LA.

124. Renee Crowley, interview, July, 14, 2007, focused on Sam Singh's role around 1996 of restoring the course.

125. Susan Fornoff, *San Francisco Chronicle*, August 11, 1999.

126. Oakland's Lake Chabot (1923), Alameda's Chuck Corica–North Course (1927) and Antioch's Lone Tree (1934) are the only public courses older than Tilden.

Chapter 7

127. Jack Burroughs, "Your Townsmen" *Oakland Tribune*, December 1, 1957.

128. Early California legislation enabled anyone to confiscate property if they intended to use it for providing water to the surrounding community.

129. Johnson, "So We're Told." According to the column, as a young boy in the 1880s, James Curran used to climb those fruit trees. In 1949, James had a contract with the university to plow up its experimental gardens.

130. Jack Burroughs, "Your Town Scribe," *Oakland Tribune*, July 19, 1953.

131. "Opening of Lake Anza," *Oakland Tribune*, May 7, 1939.

132. *Oakland Tribune*, May 25, 1947.

133. *Oakland Tribune*, August 21, 1952.

134. Attendance figures provided by Pete DeQuincy, Regional Parks aquatics manager.

Chapter 8

135. The report of Bruno's death was from a Contra Costa County newspaper dated September 25, 1970, provided by the Berkeley Historical Society.
136. Michael Grey and Anne Schnoebelen, "A Fair to Remember," *San Francisco Examiner*, April 19, 1992.
137. "Largest Artificial Island Houses Fair," *Oakland Tribune*, May 23, 1940. An archipelago in Dubai in the UAE currently holds this title.
138. Burroughs, "Your Town Scribe," provides Brazil Room history.
139. "Brazilian Room, Gift of Treasure Island, Opened and Dedicated in Tilden Park Here," *Oakland Tribune*, May 19, 1941.
140. "Soldiers to Relax at Tilden Park," *Oakland Tribune*, May 8, 1941.
141. Coverage of Lindsay's music concerts between 1941 and 1950 was provided by the *Berkeley Gazette* and *Oakland Tribune* (EBRPD archives).
142. For more information about the Brazil room, see www.ebparks.org/activities/corpfamily/br.
143. Booking statistics for 2016 through 2017 provided by Sarah Lamborn, manager of the facility.

Chapter 9

144. Professor McMinn had been hired by Amelia Reinhardt and August Vollmer in 1937 to serve as a botanic consultant. In 1938, Reinhardt took a one-year leave of absence to join her son, the U.S. consul in Vienna. The board appointed McMinn as her replacement. Professor Howard McMinn also was president of the California Botanical Society and a member of the advisory board of the Botanical Gardens in Santa Barbara.
145. Rimo Bacigalupi, "The Regional Parks Botanic Garden in Tilden Park," *California Horticultural Society Journal* (January 1963): 14.
146. Stephen Edwards and Wayne Roderick, "The East Bay Regional Parks Botanic Garden in Tilden Park Revisited," *Pacific Horticulture* (Summer 1992): 15.
147. "2000 Trees for Hill Park Arrive," *Berkeley Daily Gazette*, March 18, 1937.
148. Stephen Edwards, "Roof Tales, Part One," *Manzanita* 11, no. 4 (Winter 2007–8): 10.
149. Philip Ferry, "Mountain Plant Explorer," *Pacific Discovery* (November–December 1957): 25–29.

150. Alice Howard, "Obituary: James B. Roof 1910–1983," *California Native Society* (April 1983).

151. Edwards, "Roof Tales, Part One," 11.

152. Stephen Edwards, "Roof Tales, Part Two," *Manzanita* 12, no. 2 (Summer 2008): 11.

153. Stephen Edwards, "A Refuge for Plants, Birds, and People," *Manzanita* 1, no. 1 (Summer 1997): 3.

154. The UC Jepson Herbarium established in 1950 specializes in the vascular plants of California.

155. Stephen Edwards, "The First Friends," *Manzanita* 7, no. 2 (Summer 2003).

156. Jerry Kent, "Botanic Garden Controversy of 1965, and the Founding of CNPS," *Manzanita* 19, no. 1, 2 (Winter/Spring 2015).

157. Howard Obituary.

158. See California Native Plant Society website, http://cnps.org.

159. EBRPD Public Affairs news release, June 1976.

160. EBRPD Public Affairs Press release by Grace Lewis and Monte Monteagle, 1976.

161. Stephen Edwards, "Wayne Roderick: Still Plant-Happy After All These Years" *Manzanita* 6, no. 4 (Winter 2003).

162. Stephen Edwards and Wayne Roderick, "Botanical Garden Revisited," *Pacific Horticulture* 53, no. 2 (Summer 1992): 19–21.

163. Stephen Edwards, "The Garden's Role in Cultivar Introduction," *Manzanita* 5, no. 3 (Fall 2001).

164. Bart O'Brien autobiography is quoted from a Botanic Garden newsletter, *Manzanita: Friends of the Regional Parks Botanic Garden* (Spring 2014).

Chapter 10

165. The last CCC Camp in Wildcat Canyon was Company 5498.

166. "Yanks Operate Convalescent Camp," *Oakland Post Enquirer*, August 11, 1944.

167. "Rifle Range Planned Here," *Berkeley Gazette*, July 4, 1940, discusses acquisition of 175 acres in Wildcat Canyon adjoining the nature area and its use as a training area and rifle range. Purchase price of the 175 acres was $13,900.

168. Attu and Kiska were the Aleutian Islands that were briefly (June 6, 1942 to July 28, 1943) occupied by the Japanese. See wikipedia.org/wiki/Japanese occupation_of_Kiska.

169. The Berkeley Radar installation was one of three such centers on the Pacific coast. The others were in Los Angeles and Seattle.

170. "Huge Air Control Station Revealed," *Berkeley Daily Gazette*, August 27, 1945; "Radar Center in Tilden Park was Watch Dog in War," *Oakland Tribune*, August 28, 1945.

171. "Guard Units to Take Over Anti-Aircraft Units in A-Bomb Defense Unit," *Oakland Tribune*, October 23, 1953.

172. "National Guardsmen Serve Defense Guns in Bay Hills," *Oakland Tribune*, February 4, 1957.

173. Randy Cava, "The Missiles in Our Backyard," *The Forge* 22, no.4 (Fall 2006) provides a thorough history of the East Bay's Nike history.

174. Resource Analysis of Wildcat Canyon and Charles Lee Tilden, November 1975.

175. Cava, "Missiles in Our Backyard."

176. "Haunted Village Will Be Razed," *Oakland Tribune*, June 7, 1973.

177. EBRPD news release, August 2, 1971.

178. See http://berkeleyrotary.org/berkeley-rotary-peace-grove-recipients.php.

Chapter 11

179. Redwood Park opened in 1939 after the acquisition of 1,057 acres from EBMUD. No new regional parks were acquired until Roberts Park in 1951.

180. J.I.B. Jones, current manager of Griffith Park Golf Course, provided the account to author: Bell & Johnson's work in Griffith Park between 1933 and 1937 included the remaking of the nine-hole Roosevelt Municipal Course. The course was demolished for the expansion of the zoo in the summer of 1964 and later rebuilt at another site within Griffith Park.

181. The American Federation of State, County and Municipal Employees.

182. "Park Firings Cause Row in East Bay," *San Francisco Chronicle*, March 21, 1959.

183. Regional park board minutes from 1960 to 1961.

184. "Heart Attack Fatal to Park Supervisor," *Valley Times* (North Las Vegas) obituary column, October 9, 1973.

185. "Diary of Richard Walpole 1937–39."

Chapter 12

186. Jane Grey, "Fall Brings Football—and Dave Snyder, Too," *Oakland Tribune*, September 29, 1946.

187. Jane Grey, "Dream Camp Becomes an Actuality," *Oakland Tribune*, February 16, 1947.

188. Details of Mr. Meese's experience drawn from the 8/25/10 phone interview by author.

189. *Berkeley Daily Gazette*, April 12, 1947, quote re: CCC Camp Wildcat: "There was a dispensary, museum, library, auditorium, classroom, nursery, supply shed, tool shed, garage, two living quarters, four barracks buildings and most popular of all with the youngsters, the mess hall."

190. Richard Walpole, "A Study and Report Concerning the Natural Area in Tilden Regional Park," August 22, 1948, EBRPD archives.

191. Jane Grey, "Tilden Park Nature Camp Reconstruction Progresses," *Oakland Tribune*, October 21, 1947.

192. "Nature Area Opens July 16," *Oakland Tribune*, June 17, 1949.

193. "68,000 Enjoy Tilden Wildlife Area," *Oakland Tribune*, June 25, 1950.

194. "Three New Clubs Open to Nature Lovers," *Oakland Tribune*, September 14, 1949. The three new clubs were the Junior Rangers, Senior Rangers and the Camera Club.

195. Glenn and Wendy Rogers, now living in South Pasadena, were both interviewed by author in January 2016.

196. December 11, 1997 EBRPD news release about the December 22 event.

197. "Camp Tahloma Open for Nature Classes," *Oakland Tribune*, October 9, 1949.

198. "Junior Rangers Dedicate New Museum," *Oakland Tribune*, July 15, 1956.

199. "Teachers Oppose School Budget Cuts," *Oakland Tribune*, March 15, 1966.

200. "Building Devoted to Study of the Environment," *Oakland Tribune*, October 27,1974. According to Alan Kaplan, there was a small niche to put samples of wildflowers on display in glass vials of water dedicated to Boots Parker.

201. *San Leandro Morning News*, October 1, 1962; *Oakland Tribune*, March 21, 1965; EBRPD biography; October 22, 2008 press release from National Association for Interpretation.

202. "EEC: Building Devoted to Studying the Environment," *Oakland Tribune*, October 27, 1974.

203. Quotes from a 2009 interview and emails.
204. Steve Abbors, interview with the author, February 2016.
205. Quotes from February 2016 email.
206. Quotes from author interviews in 2007 and 2014.
207. Quotes from the EBRPD website.
208. TNA statistics provided by Kim Spinale on behalf of Sara Fetterly.

Chapter 13

209. According to the National Carousel Association's census of 2011, out of nearly 5,000 classic wooden carousels manufactured in the United States, 204 are still in operation, of which 98 are from four Herschell-Spillman companies.
210. Jerry Kent, interview with the author.
211. Terri Oyarzun, interview with the author.
212. Goats-R-Us business today is operated by their son Zephyr.
213. The ninety-five-page book by Richard Langs is available for sale at the Tilden Merry-go-round.

Chapter 14

214. Erich Thomsen story and Redwood Valley Railway history provided by Ellen Thomsen.
215. Sam Zuckerman, "Faces of Labor," *San Francisco Chronicle*, September 3, 2007.
216. Rick Del Vecchio, "Tilden Miniature Railroad Celebrates 50 Years in Berkeley," *San Francisco Chronicle*, June 1, 2002.
217. Sixty live steam railroad clubs in the country are listed on the railroaddata.com website.
218. Victor's early story and portrait taken from ibs.org website.
219. Club history and photographs were provided by Stan James.
220. Board minutes dated August 28, 1948, per resolution no.1065, describe park invitation to GGLS to use Redwood Park site.
221. "Land Given for Model Rail Line," *Oakland Tribune*, March 13, 1949.

Chapter 15

222. William Penn Mott, "Dynamic Park Leadership, 1962–1967," interview by Mimi Stein, July 17, 1981, EBRPD archives.
223. David Napier, "First Employee of the East Bay Regional Park Retires," *Oakland Tribune*, 1971.
224. Karana Hattersley-Drayton, "A Career Perspective, William Penn Mott Oral History," December 27, 1990, EBRPD archives.
225. Ibid.
226. Mott, "Dynamic Park Leadership."
227. Composition and results of four committees extracted from EBRPD board minutes between August 1962 and June 1964.

Chapter 16

228. Steve Edwards, "A Meditation on East Bay Natural History at First Contact," *Four Seasons* 10, no. 3 (December 1997); Jerry Kent, "How the East Bay Got Its Eucalyptus and Pine Forests, and the Benefits and Responsibilities of Owning Urban Forests," February 8, 2016, EBRPD archives [unpublished].
229. Kent, "How the East Bay."
230. According to the district, the 2010 Federal Plan is consistent with the district's master plan and built upon the district's ongoing fuels management activities, as well as the 1982 Blue Ribbon Report, the 1995 Fire Hazard Mitigation Program and Fuel Management Plan for the East Bay Hills (1995 plan) and other district plans and policies.
231. EBRPD Public Affairs news release, May 12, 2015.
232. Ibid.
233. Estimate per 2014 Fuel Management Program of Work and Fuels Cost Analysis EBRPD report, August 14, 2013.
234. Rachel McDonald, interview with the author, February 22, 2016.
235. Jeff Wilson quotes from "Making Their Mark, A Generation that Shaped EBRPD," *Bay Nature*, May 2014.
236. Davio Santos biography from Jerry Kent, June 2016.
237. Sergio Huerta, interview with the author, June 2016.

Chapter 17

238. Statistics provided by EBRPD Public Affairs Department.

ABOUT THE AUTHOR

After retiring from a thirty-year career providing financial expertise to the transportation industry, Richard returned to his two favorite hobbies, photography and golf. Tilden Regional Park Golf Course became the center of his new world. He has run the all-volunteer Ambassador Program at the Tilden course for the past decade and has provided his photographic skills for Northern California charity events run by local golf course operators. He lives in Oakland, California.